AN ANTHOLOGY
OF INTRIGUING

Animals

Written by Ben Hoare

Illustrated by Daniel Long,
Angela Rizza, and Daniela Terrazzini

Contents

Baleen whale...................................4

Orca...6

Elephant...8

Crocodile.......................................10

Shark...12

Giraffe...14

Rhinoceros.....................................16

Hippopotamus................................18

Jellyfish..20

Cobra...22

Tiger..24

Dolphin..26

Lion...28

Walrus..30

Peafowl..32

Camel..34

Moose..36

Swordfish.......................................38

Polar bear......................................40

Ostrich...42

Puma...44

Zebra...46

Kangaroo.......................................48

Snow leopard.................................50

Boa..52

Cheetah...54

Anteater...56

Reindeer...58

Stingray..60

African wild dog..............................62

Giant panda...................................64

Wolf...66

Gorilla..68

Milk snake......................................70

Seal...72

Sheep...74

Otter..76

Marine iguana................................78

Orangutan......................................80

Wolverine.......................................82

Flamingo..84

Octopus..86

Red panda......................................88

Beaver..90

Sea turtle..92

Pheasant..94

Penguin..96

Porcupine..98

Mandrill..100

Pangolin..102

Lemur...104

Vulture..106

Raccoon..108

Bat...110

Skunk	112	
Salmon	114	
Parrot	116	
Quokka	118	
Squirrel monkey	120	
Viscacha	122	
Parrotfish	124	
Koala	126	
Owl	128	
Sloth	130	
Fox	132	
Hare	134	
Kiwi	136	
Platypus	138	
Chameleon	140	
Gila monster	142	
Meerkat	144	
Piranha	146	
Toucan	148	
Tortoise	150	
Caecilian	152	
Flying fish	154	
Gecko	156	
Seadragon	158	
Puffin	160	
Viperfish	162	
Hedgehog	164	
Starfish	166	
Axolotl	168	
Slow loris	170	
Toad	172	
Moth	174	
Mole	176	
Hummingbird	178	
Scorpion	180	
Mantis shrimp	182	
Butterfly	184	
Kingfisher	186	
Sea slug	188	
Clownfish	190	
Dragonfly	192	
Frog	194	
Grasshopper	196	
Praying mantis	198	
Crab	200	
Beetle	202	
Ant	204	
Bug	206	
Wasp	208	
Spider	210	
Tree of life	212	
Glossary	214	
Visual guide	216	
Acknowledgments	224	

Baleen whale

Some humpbacks will blow a bubble ring
around a shoal of fish, herding them together
so the whale can eat them in one mouthful.

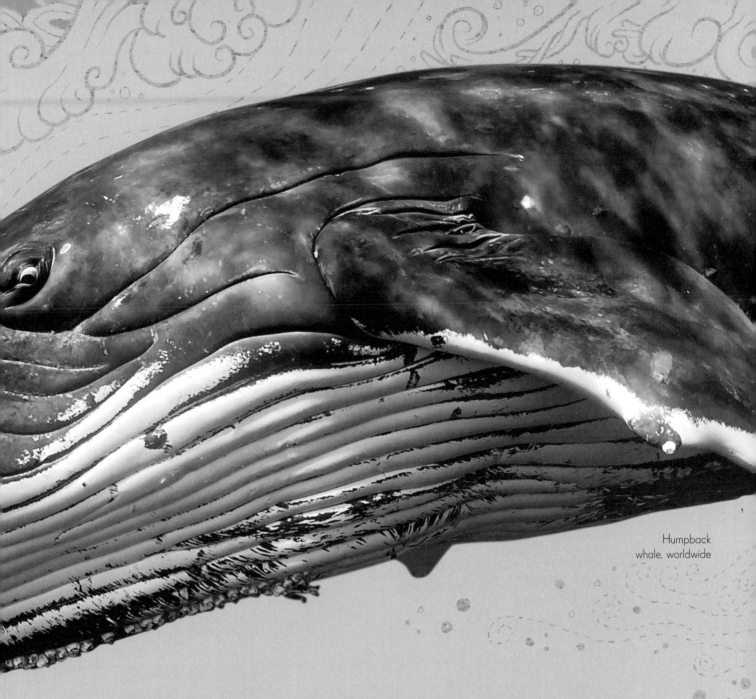

Humpback
whale, worldwide

Out in the big blue ocean, whales spend their lives swimming around underwater. However, as mammals, they have to come to the surface to breathe. To help with this, their nostrils have moved onto the top of their head. The jet of spray they make when they breathe out of their blowhole can be as high as a house.

Baleen whales, such as humpback whales, don't have teeth. Instead, they have long bristles called baleen, which filter small fish and shrimp from the water like a kitchen strainer. Their huge babies drink milk, though. A newborn calf drinks enough milk every day to fill a bathtub!

Orca

Orca, worldwide

Don't try this yourself, but orcas can swim
half asleep! One side of their brain takes a nap
while the other side stays awake.

Orcas are often called killer whales, but they aren't really whales. They are giant black-and-white dolphins. How confusing! These speedy hunters live in families called pods. Many pods only catch fish, but other pods catch seals, whales, and other dolphins. Some push waves over floating blocks of ice to wash seals into the sea.

Orcas are very chatty animals that talk with whistles and clicks. The orcas in each part of the ocean sound different. In an aquarium, some orcas learned to copy humans, saying "hello" and "good-bye." However, many people think orcas should not be in zoos and belong in the ocean.

Elephant

An elephant can look in a mirror and recognize itself.
Not many animals can do that!

It is said that elephants never forget, and it's true! They remember the faces of other elephants they have not seen for years. Elephants use their flexible trunk to smell and breathe, just like we use our nose. However, we don't use our nose to pick up food, drink, scratch, or give hugs, and elephants do. A trunk is a hose, too. If you're a hot elephant, there is no better way to cool off than to squirt water on your back.

The African bush elephant is the heaviest of all land animals, and it has the biggest front teeth—tusks! In an elephant family, the biggest female is boss. This mighty mother leads the others to food and water.

African bush elephant, Africa

Crocodile

Saltwater crocodile,
Southeast Asia and Australia

Scientists think some crocodiles can live more than one hundred years, and that they never stop growing—they just keep getting bigger.

Is that a floating log? Or a crocodile? Make a mistake and you could be dinner! Crocodiles lie low in muddy water so only their eyes and nostrils show. They wait patiently until an animal comes too near the water's edge, then ... snap! Crocs gobble everything from fish to water buffalo. There is a story that crocodiles cry when eating. People used to think it was made-up, but now we know it's true! The crocs aren't sad, though. The water is squeezed out when they bite.

Saltwater crocodiles are the largest reptiles. Although they look scary, they can be very gentle. Mother crocodiles carefully carry their babies around in their mouth.

Great hammerhead,
worldwide

Shark

Sharks may have a fearsome reputation, but they are much more interested in fish than in us. In fact, sharks are more intriguing than scary. A tiny lantern shark could fit in an adult's hand and can glow in the dark, while the whale shark is as large as a truck, but eats nothing bigger than shrimp.

One of the strangest-looking of all the sharks is the hammerhead. Its eyes and nostrils are at either end of its T-shaped head! The shark moves its head from side to side, using it to feel for the faint electrical signals made by prey. Once found, the fish don't stand a chance—the hammerhead's razor-sharp teeth soon finish the job!

Many sharks will grow and lose thousands of teeth over their lifetime. As the old teeth fall out, new ones move to the front.

Giraffe

Measuring up to 20 ft (6 m) from head to toe, giraffes are the world's tallest animals. They could easily peek into a second-floor bedroom window! Everything about a giraffe is huge. Its feet are about the size of dinner plates, and its giant heart is almost 40 times the weight of a human's. Giraffes are even big enough for other animals to live on. Oxpecker birds cling to their fur and search for bloodsucking ticks to eat.

Being tall has its problems. To drink, giraffes almost have to do splits to get their head down to the water, and giving birth standing up is tricky. A newborn giraffe has a 7 ft (2 m) fall to the ground.

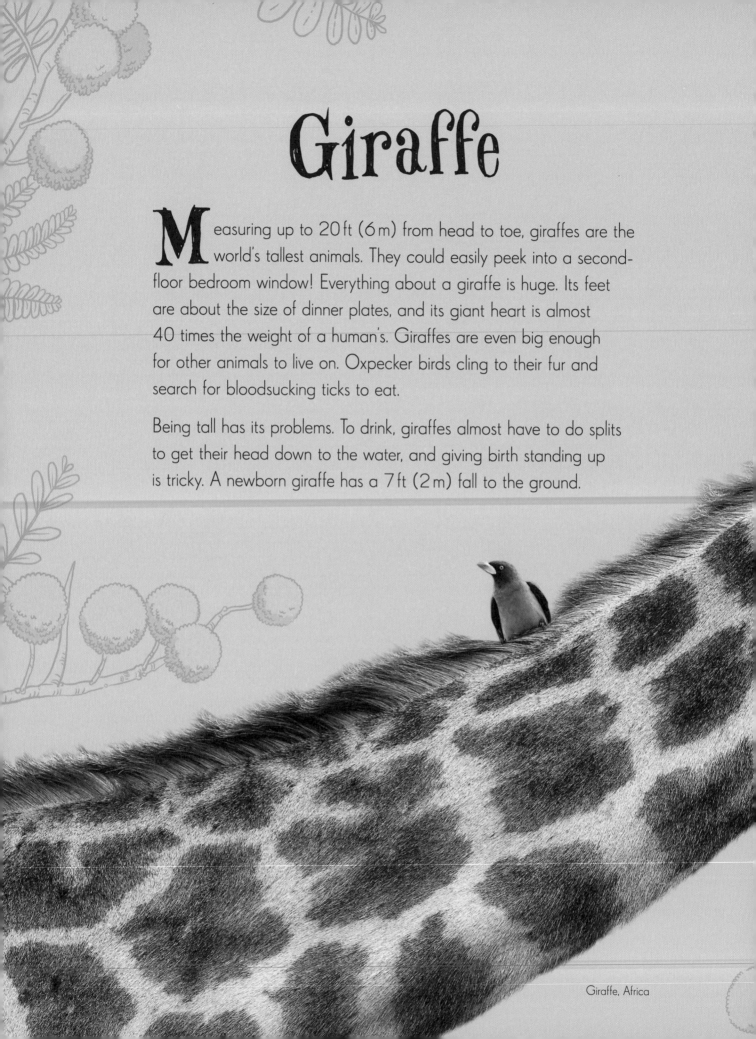

Giraffe, Africa

Giraffes use their long, leathery tongues
to strip the leaves off thorny
acacia trees.

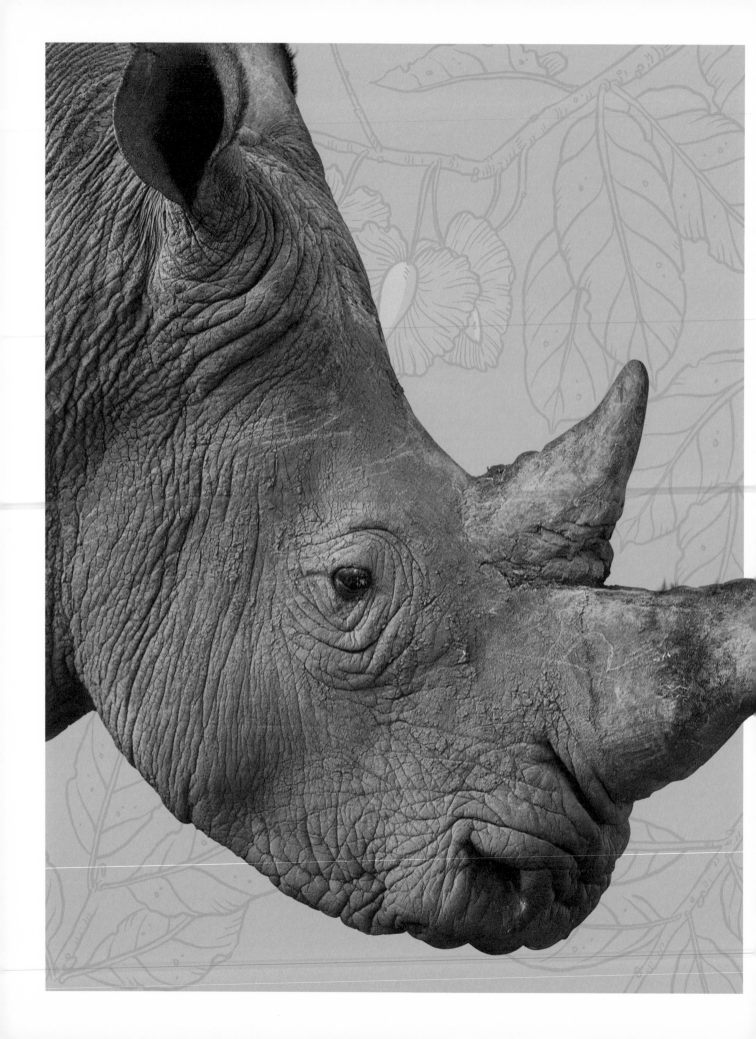

Rhinoceros

A rhino has fantastic hearing.
Its cup-shaped ears help it catch sounds.

Rhinoceros means "nose horn." There are five species of rhino, some with one horn and others with two. Unfortunately, their horns are the reason why these huge herbivores have been hunted almost to extinction. Some people believe rhinoceros horn works as a medicine, but it is made from the same material as human hair and nails.

The white rhinoceros is found grazing in the savannas of Africa. Rhinos eat a lot and can dump more than 44 lb (20 kg) of dung a day! Every rhino's dung smells different, and their piles of poop can send smelly messages to each other.

White rhinoceros,
southern Africa

17

Hippopotamus

Muddy puddles are the place to be if you're a common hippopotamus. It's the best way for this giant to keep cool in the scorching sun. The name hippopotamus comes from an Ancient Greek word that means "river horse," but this water-loving mammal is more closely related to whales and dolphins than horses.

Common hippos are quite bad-tempered. If you disturb one, it yawns to show off its tusklike front teeth as a warning. If you really annoy it, it will charge. It may be a vegetarian, but this is one of Africa's most dangerous animals! In the cool of the night, hippos leave the water to munch grass, moving around like herds of giant lawn mowers.

The hippopotamus sweats a kind of thick, pink slime over its skin, which works as sunscreen.

Common hippopotamus, Africa

Pacific sea nettle,
eastern Pacific Ocean

Jellyfish

Jellyfish go with the flow, drifting through the sea wherever the current takes them. Their soft bodies do not have a brain, heart, or bones. In fact, they are nearly all water. Their round top is called a bell and their long arms dangle below it like spaghetti. These arms are packed with stingers that stun fish or plankton. Once prey is caught, the arms pull it up to the bell, where a mouth is hidden.

Jellyfish start life attached to the seabed. They release many baby jellyfish, which float away and begin to grow. If there is lots of food, the jellyfish multiply fast. This is called a bloom. Blooms may have billions of jellyfish in them!

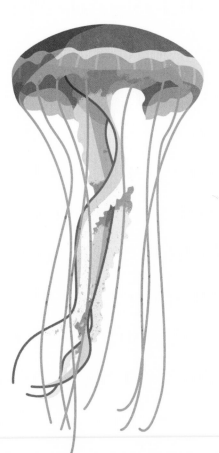

The Pacific sea nettle's tentacles can be longer than a boa constrictor!

King cobra,
Southeast Asia

Cobra

The king cobra is the world's longest venomous snake. It is the length of three human adults put together, and just one bite contains enough venom to kill twenty people. Fortunately, their favorite food is other snakes.

Cobras have a superpower—to appear bigger than they are. They bring the front part of their body up into a "standing" position. At the same time they spread their ribs and suck air into their lungs to form a hood. King cobras can "stand" 5 ft (1.5 m) tall! Some religions tell stories about legendary cobras called nagas, which can have more than one head and turn into humans.

It is a myth that all snakes hiss— king cobras growl like angry dogs!

Unlike some cats, tigers enjoy water.
They are strong swimmers and love to lie down
in rivers and lakes to cool off.

Tiger

When prowling through tall trees and waving grass, the tiger's beautiful striped fur is the perfect disguise. Tigers are the world's largest, most powerful cats. They hunt alone, often at night. Hidden by their coat, tigers wait patiently for a deer or buffalo to pass. They pounce suddenly, biting their prey's throat and holding on until it is dead. However, most hunts fail—it's not easy being a tiger.

Tigers were once found all over south Asia, but people have hunted them and cut their forests down, making them endangered. Today, most live in India. In the Hindu religion, the goddess Durga is sometimes shown riding a tiger.

Tiger, eastern Asia, southern Asia, and Southeast Asia

Dolphin

Dolphins are the biggest show-offs in the sea. They are very intelligent animals and always seem to have time to play. You often see them jump into the air or race beside boats. They love games of tag and trying to balance seaweed on their noses. Sometimes they blow giant bubbles underwater. It certainly looks like they're having fun!

Bottlenose dolphins stick close together. Each family has two to fifteen dolphins, and if one of them is hurt or sick, the others help it. Dolphins hunt with sound. They make clicks, which echo off objects so they can build a sound picture of everything around them.

Common bottlenose dolphin,
worldwide

A dolphin can send out
one thousand clicks a
second to help it find fish.

**A male lion's mane gets bigger
and darker as he gets older.**

Lioness

Lion

Lion

In many books and movies, the lion is "king of the beasts." The ancient Egyptians had a warrior goddess with the head of a lioness, and some of the oldest cave paintings are of lions. Lions form groups called prides, which are made up mainly of lionesses and their cubs. One to three males also join the pride, but only for a few years.

Lionesses are faster than male lions, so the females team up to hunt. Often they set traps for prey—one trick is to surprise animals as they drink at a water hole. All lions can roar, and they figure out how big other prides are by how many different roars they hear.

Lion, Africa
and western India

Walrus, the Arctic

Walrus

Swimming among blocks of sea ice in the Arctic Ocean is no problem for a walrus. In water this cold, we would freeze in minutes, but the wrinkly walrus has a layer of fat around it to keep it warm. It is the only seal with tusks, and these help the walrus hook onto floating ice and heave its great body out of the water. Males also have tusk fights, and many are covered in old cuts and scratches.

The Inuit people of North America have a legend that walruses and other sea mammals were first created from the fingers of a beautiful girl named Sedna. She fell out of a kayak and became a sea goddess.

Walruses use their huge moustaches to feel the muddy seabed for shellfish.

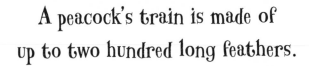

A peacock's train is made of
up to two hundred long feathers.

Peafowl

Peacock

Peahen

A male peafowl, called a peacock, has a train of fabulous feathers. He fans it out, then twirls and bows down so that the eyelike spots on it shimmer. He is trying to catch the attention of a female, called a peahen. She will choose the male with the biggest, brightest train, so although it makes it hard to fly, he grows a train up to 5 ft (1.6 m) long!

The males of the Indian peafowl are blue and green, and the females are mostly brown. However, sometimes a peafowl is born with all white feathers. Peacocks can be very noisy. The males scream "Ah-ahh!" at the top of their voice, often in the middle of the night.

Indian peafowl,
southern Asia

Camel

The question is, does it have one hump or two? A one-humped camel is called a dromedary or Arabian camel, while a camel with two humps is a Bactrian camel. Both of them are best suited to life in extreme desert conditions. Their humps store fat for when there is little water or food, and wide feet stop them from sinking in soft desert sand. Long eyelashes and closing nostrils prevent sand from getting into their eyes and nose.

For thousands of years, dromedary camels have transported people and goods across hot deserts. However, they can get grumpy, so beware—they might spit at you!

A camel can drink 22 gallons (100 liters) in just ten minutes. That's like drinking a glass of water every two seconds!

Dromedary camel, northern Africa and the Arabian Peninsula

Moose

Moose, North America,
Europe, and northern Asia

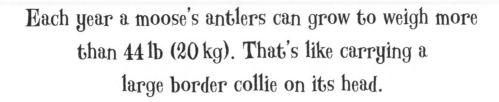

Each year a moose's antlers can grow to weigh more than 44 lb (20 kg). That's like carrying a large border collie on its head.

See that lump under the moose's chin? To us, it looks pretty strange, but to a female moose, it looks great—so the male moose gives it a wobble to show off. He also impresses with his huge antlers. Antlers are made of bone and, amazingly, they are replaced every year. They grow in summer, then drop off again in winter.

Moose are the largest deer in the world. They eat leaves and water plants, but in winter they live mainly on twigs. That's right: tasty twigs! They are great swimmers, and in summer moose love to soak in lakes. Bears and wolves are their main enemies. Moose kick them with sharp hooves to drive them away.

Imagine having a nose the length of a tennis racket! The swordfish's long beak is actually part of its upper jawbone, and it has a sharp point, just like a sword. You won't be surprised to learn that it is used to kill prey, but probably not in the way you think. Rather than using its pointed bill to spear smaller fish, a swordfish slashes its prey with the sword's sharp edges. The meal is swallowed whole because, amazingly, this terrifying fish has no teeth!

Swordfish have a special system that keeps their eyes and brain warm in cold water. This helps them see and hunt for food. Favorite snacks include tuna and squid.

Swordfish

Adult swordfish don't have many predators.
Only a really fast hunter, such as an orca,
will try and take them on.

Swordfish, worldwide

A polar bear may eat 99 lb (45 kg) of seal meat in one meal, but can go six months without any food.

Polar bear,
the Arctic

Polar bear

The polar bear is a giant. It can weigh about 1,750 lb (800 kg) and its huge feet leave footprints larger than dinner plates. Super-thick fur keeps the bear cozy in its Arctic home. The fur looks as white as snow, but it is actually see-through! It just seems white because of the way each hair reflects light. Underneath, the bear's skin is black—this helps it soak up the sun's rays to stay warm.

These bears crunch across snow and paddle in icy water for days, hunting for seals to eat. They use their nose to sniff out underground seal dens. If they find one, they have to dig out the seal quickly before it escapes.

An ostrich would beat you in a race, however hard you tried! In short bursts ostriches can reach 43 mph (70 kph). These feathered giants are the tallest, heaviest birds in the world, and they can't fly. Instead, they wander across savannas and deserts on foot.

The female ostrich is brown, but the male has black and white feathers, and sometimes a bright pink neck and legs. He crouches down and swishes his wings around to impress a watching female. If she likes him she will lay her eggs in the nest he has made. People used to think that when an ostrich was frightened, it buried its head in the sand—it's a myth, though!

Ostrich

Ostriches lay enormous eggs—
each one weighs the same as
twenty-four chicken eggs!

Common ostrich,
Africa

Puma

**Pumas cannot roar, but just like
a pet cat, they can purr.**

A mysterious cat, the puma has many names, including mountain lion and cougar. Pumas live in all sorts of different habitats from mountains and forests to deserts and swamps, but they are rarely seen by humans. They are often caught only by hidden cameras—one camera even captured a puma walking past the famous Hollywood sign in the hills above Los Angeles, California.

Pumas have a special place in the history of the Americas. They appear in many Native American and early South American stories and artworks. Unfortunately, these beautiful animals have been hunted for their fine fur. Today, the puma is protected in most countries where it lives.

Puma, North, Central, and South America

Zebra

Is a zebra black with white stripes? Or white with black stripes? You decide! Every zebra's pattern is different, just like a bar code. It used to be thought that the stripes made it more difficult for predators to catch a zebra. However, it's now thought that the black and white bars might prevent bites from flies, because these insects avoid striped surfaces.

Zebras are wild horses that live in the wide savannas of Africa. One story told by the San people of southern Africa describes how the zebra got its stripes—they say it was originally white all over, but was left with scorch marks after falling into a fire.

A zebra hoof is actually a huge toenail!

Plains zebra, eastern and southern Africa

Kangaroo

In Australia, there are twice as many kangaroos as there are people. These jumping animals are tough enough to go several days without drinking in the hot deserts and dry grasslands where they live. The biggest of the kangaroos is the red kangaroo. Its massive back legs work like springs so it can leap 30 ft (9 m) at a time. Its thick tail helps it keep its balance when bouncing.

Kangaroos are marsupials, which are mammals that give birth to tiny babies. To stay safe while growing, each baby kangaroo—called a joey—rides in a pouch on its mother's tummy for eight months.

Red kangaroo,
Australia

**Kangaroos lick spit onto their arms
to help them cool down.**

A gray coat with dark spots camouflages the snow leopard against the snow and rocks.

People in the Himalayan mountains talk about the "ghost of the mountains." The ghost is the snow leopard. This secretive big cat lives among the world's highest peaks and is very hard to see. Life is tough high up. The temperature can drop to a chilly −40°F (−40°C). However, the snow leopard is built for the extreme cold. An extra-thick coat keeps it warm, and it wraps its chunky tail around itself like a scarf.

To find enough food, the snow leopard has to patrol huge areas. Mountain sheep or goats are its favorite prey. Catching them on steep slopes is tricky, but big paws help the leopard grip icy rocks.

Snow leopard

Snow leopard,
central Asia

Boa

Deep in the Amazon rain forest of South America, you'll find the emerald tree boa looped around a strong branch. This snake spends hours with its head dangling down, waiting and waiting. Rats and bats are on the menu. Not all snakes have a deadly bite: boas kill by squeezing. When a meal comes along, the boa grabs it and wraps its long body around it tightly, holding it until its victim's blood stops flowing. Its jaws open extra wide to swallow its dinner in one bite. The mysterious row of holes around the emerald tree boa's mouth are heat pits. The pits feel the warmth of any animal nearby so the snake can find food in total darkness.

Baby emerald tree boas are bright orange or red.
They turn green by the time they're a year old.

Emerald tree boa,
South America

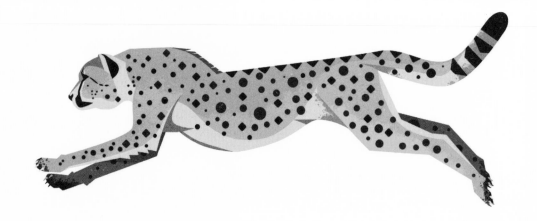

Cheetah

Cheetahs are built for speed. Their light skeleton saves weight, their leg muscles are huge, and their claws grip the ground like the spikes on football cleats. All this gives cheetahs a top speed of 70 mph (113 kph). On most roads, they would break the speed limit!

When cheetahs chase prey, they soon get hot and tired. If they have not caught up after a minute, they give up. Young male cheetahs often hunt together. Long grass makes it hard to see one another, so they keep in touch with barks and birdlike chirps. They share their meat, rub heads, and lick each other to stay friends.

A flexible backbone means a cheetah's legs can stretch far out, helping it run faster.

Cheetah, Africa

Giant anteater, Central
and South America

A giant anteater can catch
35,000 ants in a single day.

Anteater

Who needs teeth? Not anteaters. Their favorite meal of termites and ants can easily be swallowed without them, but first they have to catch these tasty critters. The giant anteater uses its strong, curved claws to punch a hole though the tough clay wall of a termite mound. Next, it flicks its gigantic tongue into the nest up to 150 times a minute. Sticky saliva and tiny spines on the tongue's surface pick up the insects inside.

Such long claws make walking difficult, so the anteater has to walk on its knuckles! When it is ready to rest, it folds its bushy tail over itself like a blanket.

Reindeer

Few animals live in the freezing Arctic, but for reindeer this world of ice and snow is home. They roam in restless herds that are always on the move, making long journeys called migrations to find fresh plants to eat. People have tamed reindeer in Russia and northern Europe. The tough animals pull sleighs and are kept for their meat and skins. Reindeer in North America are called caribou. These creatures are wilder and more afraid of humans.

Reindeer have wide feet that stop them from sinking when they crunch across the snow. You can hear them coming, as their feet make a loud clicking noise when they walk.

In most deer, only the males, called stags, have antlers. However, both male and female reindeer have them.

Stingray

Wait a minute ... is that two eyes staring at you from the ocean floor? Often the eyes of a stingray are the only parts you can see. Stingrays' round bodies are as flat as pancakes, and they love to bury themselves in the sand. Above their long tail are two spikes full of venom. However, rays don't usually sting humans, unless you step on one by mistake!

Blue-spotted ribbontail rays hunt small fish and crabs. The rays can feel the tiny electrical pulses made by the muscles of their prey, which means they're able to find food even if it is hidden from view.

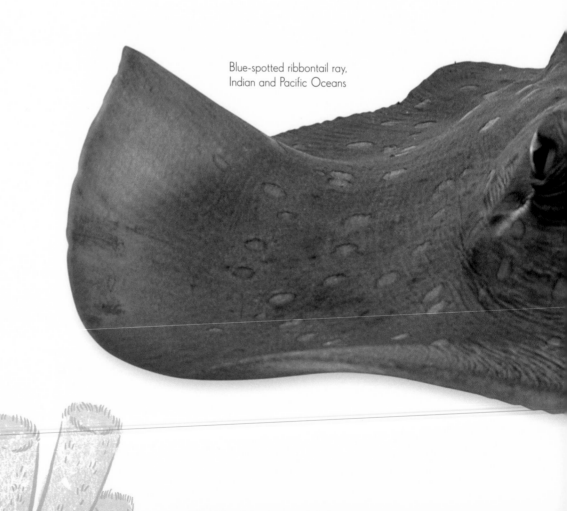

Blue-spotted ribbontail ray,
Indian and Pacific Oceans

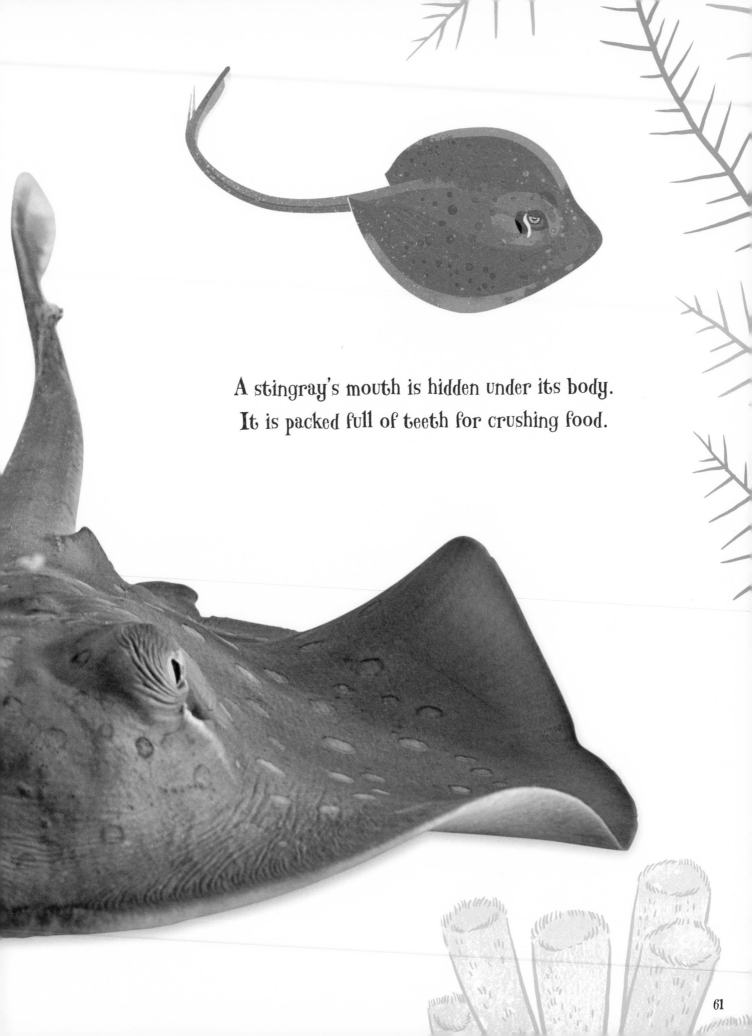

A stingray's mouth is hidden under its body.
It is packed full of teeth for crushing food.

African wild dog

African wild dog,
Africa

Africal wild dogs belong to packs that do everything together. The dogs give one another friendly licks, and stay in touch using whistles and yaps. They decide to go hunting by sneezing! When enough dogs sneeze, the pack sets off. Up to thirty dogs work as a team to hunt antelopes and other big animals. The dogs race after their prey, kicking up clouds of dust. To stop the prey from getting away, they split up, blocking every escape.

Only the pack's top female has babies. She can have as many as 12 pups in a litter. The whole pack guards them and tears up meat for the pups to eat.

Another name for the wild dog is "painted wolf" because of its patterned fur.

Giant panda

Baby pandas are born pink and have very little fur.
They grow their black-and-white coat by three weeks old.

High up in China's cool, wet mountains you might spot a giant panda. Local people call them "bamboo bears," after the panda's favorite food. Bamboo is a tall type of grass that pandas love. They spend half of every day sitting and eating. They even have a special wrist bone that works like a thumb to help them hold sticks of bamboo.

All over the world, pandas are famous because they have become so rare. To save the species, China has set up panda breeding centers, where many cubs are born. Some of the center workers dress as pandas so the cubs don't get too used to humans.

Giant panda,
China

Wolf

Arroooo! Wolves are said to howl at the moon. That isn't actually true, but wolves do howl after sunset, because they are most active in the dark. Wolves live in packs, and when one wolf starts howling all the others join in. Wolves also communicate using body language. If you're the boss, you hold your ears and tail high, but if you are junior, you crouch low, flatten your ears, and tuck your tail between your legs.

In Viking mythology there was a giant wolf called Fenrir. He was so fierce that the gods tied him up with a magical chain so he couldn't escape.

Gray wolf, North America, Europe, Asia, and the Arctic

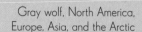

Even the tiniest pet dogs are descended from wolves that were tamed thousands of years ago.

Every person's fingerprints are different—and
every gorilla's nose print is different!

Western gorilla,
central Africa

Gorilla

Gorillas are Africa's gentle giants. These great apes are mainly vegetarian, eating leaves and fruits. An adult gorilla may munch 66 lb (30 kg) of plants a day. After eating fruits from trees, gorillas help spread the seeds—in their poop. Because of this, many forest trees depend on them.

Each gorilla family is ruled by a huge male—the silverback. His muscles are massive, and his head has a large bony lump on top. When the silverback is annoyed, he beats his chest and throws plants around. However, fights between gorillas are unusual. Baby gorillas enjoy cuddles and piggyback rides from their mother and aunts.

Milk snake

Sometimes a large milk snake
will catch a smaller one and
swallow it whole.

Milk snake, North, Central,
and South America

People used to think that this striped snake drank milk from
cows. It doesn't, but the common name "milk snake" has stuck.
It actually eats lizards, rats, and mice. Slithering through the grass,
it flicks its tongue in and out to collect smells. This is how it finds
exactly where its prey is. The milk snake doesn't have venom to kill
with, so it gulps prey down while it's still alive.

These sneaky snakes have a cunning defense, too. Their red,
black, and white pattern copies the deadly coral snake, which has
powerful venom. Other animals are tricked into thinking the milk
snake is dangerous, so they leave it alone.

Seal

The harp seal's name comes from the markings on the male's back that look a bit like the musical instrument.

Born on ice floating in the freezing Arctic Ocean, harp seals have a tough start to life. Luckily each pup has a "babygrow" of white fur to keep it warm. Its mother's milk is as rich as cream. It helps the pup create a warm layer of fat called blubber under its skin. The pups shed their fluffy coat after only three weeks.

All seals come ashore to breed. They can't walk, so they flop around on their bellies instead. Below the waves, however, a seal's flippers and smooth fur turn them into fast and stylish swimmers. In the myths of northwest Europe, seal-shaped creatures called selkies could step out of their skin and become humans.

Harp seal,
Arctic Ocean

Sheep can recognize the faces of fifty other sheep.
This is useful if they live in a big herd!

Sheep

People first farmed sheep over ten thousand years ago in Asia. Today, there are more than one billion domestic sheep on farms all over the world, but wild sheep are different. They make their home in some of the toughest places on Earth, including high, rocky peaks and blazing hot deserts. Bighorn sheep live in the mountains of North America. Males and females have horns, but the horns of the males, called rams, are much bigger and curlier. The rams use them in head-butting fights!

Sheep are one of the twelve animals linked to the Chinese calendar. People born in the year of the sheep are meant to be very kind.

Bighorn sheep,
western North America

Otter

Sleeping sea otters wrap themselves in
seaweed so they don't float away.

Few animals swim as beautifully as otters. Their webbed feet steer and give lots of power, while smooth, slippery fur allows them to glide through the water. Otters are also fantastic at fishing. Many use their long whiskers to feel nearby fish, even in dark water.

Most otters hunt in rivers and lakes. However, sea otters live on the cold coasts of the Pacific Ocean. They are the furriest animals in the world. Air trapped in their thick coat keeps them warm and helps them float as they lie on their backs. This is how they go to sleep! Sea otters like to eat prickly sea urchins and crunchy crabs. They smash open their tough shells with a favorite rock.

Sea otter, northern
Pacific Ocean

Marine iguana

Marine iguana,
Galápagos Islands
off South America

Does this iguana remind you of a dinosaur? Iguanas definitely look fierce, with their spiky scales and sharp claws. Most iguanas live in hot forests and deserts. However, unlike every other lizard on Earth, the marine iguana lives by the sea.

Marine iguanas are found only on the Galápagos Islands, near Ecuador. They eat algae, and to reach this unusual food they climb onto slippery rocks when the tide goes out. Big iguanas actually dive into the water and feed below the waves, lashing their tail from side to side to swim. They swallow a lot of seawater as they eat, and to get rid of the extra salt, they sneeze it out!

Each island's marine iguanas are a different color. Those on Española Island are brightest, with red and green scales.

Bornean orangutan,
Borneo in Southeast Asia

Orangutan

In zoos, orangutans learn to copy things we do.
They are able to saw wood and hammer nails!

Orangutan means "person of the forest." It's a good name because these orange apes don't like to leave the treetops. Orangutans swing through the trees using their long arms, looking for ripe fruits to eat. When it rains, they hold a large leaf over their head as an umbrella. Each evening they bend branches to build a new leafy nest to sleep in. Most orangutans live on their own, but mothers go everywhere with their babies, which take a long time to grow up. A baby shares its mother's nest every night for eight years. The larger males spend more time on the forest floor. You can tell a male by his unusual cheek pads.

Wolverine

Hungry wolverines gulp down the skin, feet, teeth, and bones of their prey!

Wolverine, North America, Europe, and Asia

Bounding through cold Arctic forests, the fierce wolverine is perfectly at home. Like many mammals, it wears two coats at once. On top, it has a coat of very long fur that is frost-resistant. Underneath, there is a second layer, which is super soft and super thick. Wolverines even have extra-furry feet, which act as snowshoes.

The wolverine has a powerful body and massive jaws that can crunch through bone and frozen meat. This is useful because it buries leftovers in the snow to eat later. A wolverine will eat almost anything—mice, deer, bird eggs, berries, and even uneaten prey left by other predators.

Flamingos look after their young in giant nurseries on the water. In Africa, nurseries of the lesser flamingo contain up to 300,000 chicks.

Chilean flamingo, South America

Flamingo

Imagine turning the color of your favorite food! Flamingos turn pink from eating pink shrimp or plantlike algae every day. Their fiery feathers made people in Ancient Egypt think they were a symbol of their sun god, Ra. The Egyptians even used a picture of the bird to mean the word "red."

A forest of legs in the shallow lakes of South America's Andes mountains probably belongs to a group of Chilean flamingos. These birds breed in large groups. When they are ready, they build a volcano-shaped nest from sticky brown mud. A single egg is laid on top. Once hatched, flamingo parents feed their fluffy chick with milk made in their throats. This milk is also pink!

Octopuses have blue blood and three hearts.
One heart stops beating while they swim.

Common octopus,
worldwide

Octopus

Imagine having eight arms like an octopus! It uses them to move around the sea floor, coiling and winding them around rocks. Each arm has more than two hundred white suckers that taste, feel, and stick to things like superglue! To swim, octopuses pump water through their soft body. When they squeeze the water out, they take off like a balloon zooming around a room.

Octopuses are some of the smartest animals in the ocean. The common octopus holds stones to make body armor, and in captivity it can solve puzzles and escape mazes. Sailors in northern Europe used to tell tales about a giant, octopus-like sea monster that could sink ships. They called it the "kraken."

Up to 90 percent of the red panda's food is bamboo. It especially likes new spring shoots.

Red panda

The red panda looks very cute. It has a teddy-bear face, furry coat, and bushy tail. But is it a panda? Or a bear? Neither! Scientists put the red panda in a group all on its own. However, if you think it looks like a red raccoon, you are close—raccoons are some of its closest relatives.

The red panda's home is the mountain forests of Asia. There you can hear it twittering and making a grunting noise called a "huff-quack." Its long tail helps the red panda balance on branches, and it has a special trick to help it get around—it can twist its ankles around to point backward. This allows it to climb down trees headfirst!

Red panda, Himalayan mountains and southwest China

Beaver

Bite marks on fallen trees are a clue that beavers are around. Their orange front teeth are very sharp for chewing wood, which they eat and use for construction. Beaver families are great builders. First, they block a stream, dragging branches across and pushing mud into the gaps to make a dam. Water is trapped behind the dam and makes a pond where they can swim. Their paddle-like tails and webbed feet are perfect for pushing them along.

Next, the beavers build a home called a lodge, complete with a secret underwater entrance. If a beaver sees danger, it makes a warning splash with its tail. When the others hear this, they all swim inside.

A beaver's front teeth never stop growing!
However, all that chewing wears them down,
so they don't get too long.

American beaver,
North America

Sea turtle

When it is hotter, more turtle eggs hatch
into female babies. When it's cooler,
there are more males.

Green sea turtle, tropical Atlantic, Pacific, and Indian Oceans

Sea turtles are super swimmers, with smooth shells and long flippers. They travel huge distances as they cruise through the ocean. Some sea turtles chase jellyfish, shrimp, or crabs to eat, but green sea turtles graze on sea grass, which grows on the seabed in underwater lawns. Green sea turtles get their name because their fat is green!

Female sea turtles return to the same beach where they hatched to lay their eggs. They haul themselves onto the beach at night to dig a nest in the sand. In it they lay about one hundred white eggs, which look just like ping-pong balls. Seven or eight weeks later, the tiny babies wriggle out and dash to the sea.

Pheasant

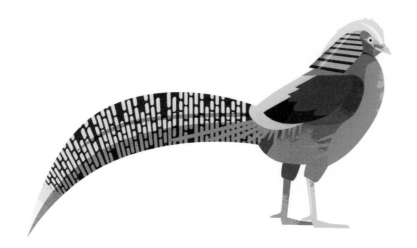

Male pheasants are some of the most dazzling birds in the world. Many are brightly colored and have long tail plumes. Golden pheasants live in dark, shady forests. If males spend too long in the sun, their feathers can lose some of their color. The female looks less eye-catching than the male, but her speckled brown feathers are the perfect disguise in dappled forest light. They hide her and her eggs from predators.

To attract a partner, a male golden pheasant puts on a special display. He dashes in front of a female and spreads his golden neck feathers to make a cape that covers his beak, leaving just enough room for him to peek over the top.

The golden pheasant lives in China, where it is a sign of beauty and good luck.

Penguin

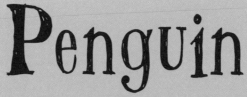

An emperor penguin can dive more than 1,640 ft (500 m) deep and hold its breath for twenty minutes.

Gentoo penguin, islands around Antarctica

Emperor penguin, Antarctica

Penguins can look clumsy as they shuffle along or slide on their bellies. They can't take to the air because their wings have become flippers, but they can zoom through the sea as if flying underwater. They even flap to push themselves along as they chase down fish and shrimplike animals called krill.

Most penguins live in the icy Southern Ocean. To stay warm, they have a thick layer of fat that traps heat, just like wearing a wetsuit! For emperor penguins, home is Antarctica—the coldest place on the planet. It's so cold, they balance their egg on their feet to keep it from freezing on the ice.

Adélie penguin, islands around Antarctica

African penguin, southern Africa

Southern rockhopper penguin, islands around Antarctica

Fairy penguin, southern Australia and New Zealand

Crested porcupine, Africa

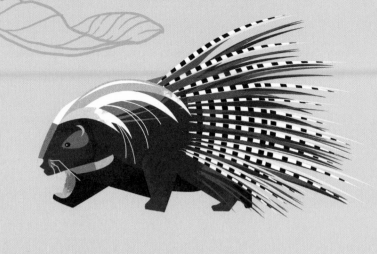

Porcupine

A spiky bush on legs! That's what a porcupine looks like. You don't want to mess with one because it has a secret weapon. Its back is covered in special stiff hairs, called quills, which are very sharp. If a porcupine is scared, it raises its quills and charges backward. Any attacker is left with a face full of spines. Ouch!

Porcupines have tiny eyes and can't see very well. Instead they sniff their way around. At night they leave their burrows to dig up roots and other plant food. They are rodents, like rats and squirrels, and like all rodents their teeth never stop growing. Some porcupines collect bones to chew on and wear their teeth down.

Porcupines rattle their quills to warn off predators.

Mandrill

The brighter a male mandrill's nose, the more important he is within his group.

With his red-and-blue face, fluffy yellow beard, and purple bottom, the male mandrill is one of the most colorful monkeys on Earth. He's also the largest. You might imagine that mandrills would be easy to find, but no. In the thick, dark African rain forests where they live, you can't see far. Instead you will mostly hear mandrills as they grunt and call to one another.

Mandrills have sharp front teeth, but these are mostly for show— they mainly eat plants and small animals. They stroll through the forest on all fours, looking for food. Female and young mandrills are small enough to climb trees, but the bigger males are too heavy.

Mandrill,
central Africa

Pangolin

Some pangolins' claws are strong enough to excavate soil that is as hard as concrete!

For many years, pangolins had people puzzled. What were these strange creatures? Lizards? Now we know that they are the only mammal covered in scales. If a pangolin is attacked, it rolls into a tight ball to shield itself. Its scales act like a suit of armor. Even lions struggle to unroll them.

The ground pangolin plods along on its back legs because of its huge, powerful front claws. Like a digger, it can quickly scoop out soil to make a burrow. At night, it goes on raids. It rips open rock-hard ant or termite nests to reach the juicy insects inside. Pangolins don't have teeth, but their long, sticky tongue is perfect for slurping up their dinner.

Ground pangolin,
Africa

Lemur

Lemurs live on the tropical island of Madagascar, off the east coast of Africa. Some are like tiny mice, but others look more like monkeys. Many of them can leap from tree to tree using their long arms and tails for balance. Ring-tailed lemurs are unusual—they often scamper across the ground of their dry forest home, their striped tails held high.

Being in a crowd suits ring-tailed lemurs. Up to thirty family members live together with a top female in charge. The gang go looking for juicy fruit, flowers, and leaves to eat, and they can't resist sap, a sweet liquid from trees. At night, the family snuggles up to sleep in a tree or cave.

Ring-tailed lemur, Madagascar

Male ring-tailed lemurs have stink fights!
They rub their tails on smelly patches in their
fur, then wave them at each other.

Vulture

Sometimes vultures eat so much they're too heavy to fly!

A group of vultures circling overhead is a sign that there is an animal carcass nearby. These birds ride warm air currents, wheeling around while scanning the ground for their preferred food—dead animals. Their massive beak helps them tear meat and snap bones as they squabble with one another to get the best scraps.

Many vultures are bald. Feathers on their face would get covered in blood when they poke their snakelike neck into bodies. Their naked head also helps them stay a good temperature whether it is hot or cold. People often think vultures are dirty, but without their help clearing away carcasses, our world would be a messier place.

Rüppell's vulture,
northern and
eastern Africa

Raccoon

Raccoons often go fishing. They know how to scoop fish right out of the water!

If you look at a raccoon, you'll see it looks like it's wearing a mask. These playful mammals are very clever with their hands. They can open doors, flip lids off boxes, and get inside trash cans. Some of them even steal people's picnics or enter houses to steal food! A raccoon is happy to eat almost anything it can find.

Raccoons are common in Canada and the USA. In the past, they mostly lived in woods and grassy places, but now many of them have moved into towns. Raccoons are good climbers, so they can scurry up walls to make their home in lofts and attics. At night, they growl and chatter, and some people think these bold animals are pests.

Lyle's flying fox,
Southeast Asia

Bat

Many people think bats are spooky, and children and adults dress as them for Halloween, but bats are amazing animals. They are the only mammals that can fly. The flaps of skin between their fingers turn their hands into wings. At night, insect-eating bats make high-pitched squeaks that bounce off moths and other insects. The echoes help the bats find them.

Not all bats eat insects. Flying foxes are giant bats that love fruit, especially mangoes and bananas. By day they sleep upside down, wrapping their wings around themselves like a blanket. Groups of them hang from branches like decorations on a Christmas tree!

A Lyle's flying fox has a wingspan of 35 in (90 cm)— that's wider than many doorways.

Striped skunk,
North America

Skunk

Skunks can hit a target 10 ft (3 m) away with their stink bomb.

You might think a fluffy skunk would be nice to pet, but you'd get a terrible surprise if you tried. The skunk's white stripes are a warning for bigger animals to leave it alone. If a predator approaches it, the skunk squirts a smelly yellow liquid from under its tail. This stinky spray can make its attackers sick or even blind them for a while, and the awful smell lasts several weeks!

Skunks prefer not to spray, so first they give extra warnings. They hiss and stamp their feet, wave their white tail around, and dance around doing handstands. Usually their enemies get the message and leave.

Sockeye salmon start their big swim home as silver fish, but finish bright red with a green head.

Sockeye salmon, Pacific Ocean

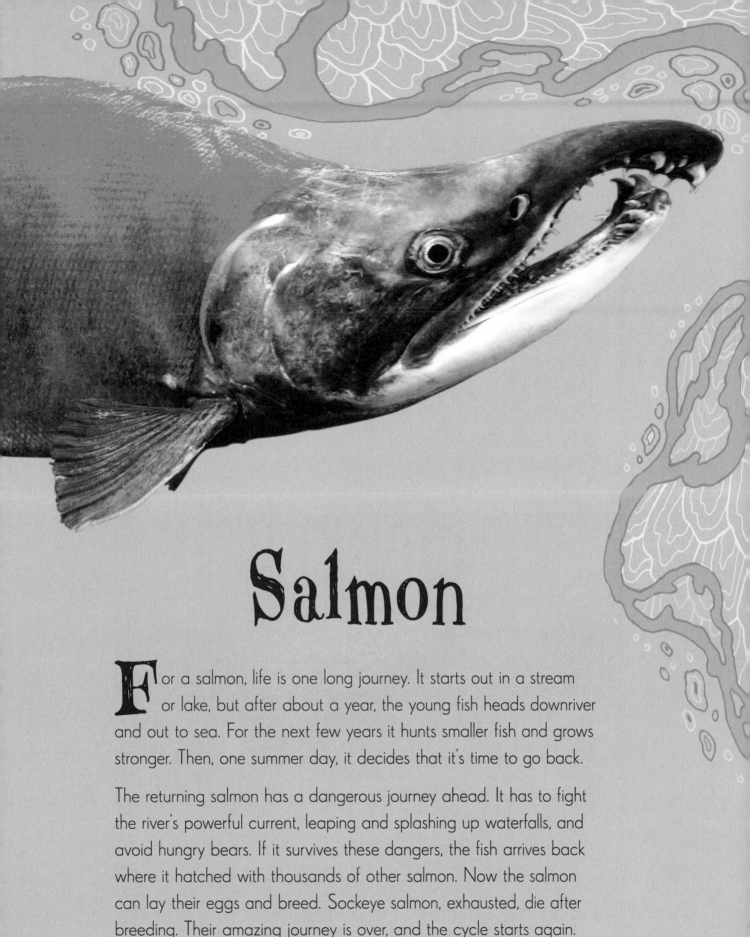

Salmon

For a salmon, life is one long journey. It starts out in a stream or lake, but after about a year, the young fish heads downriver and out to sea. For the next few years it hunts smaller fish and grows stronger. Then, one summer day, it decides that it's time to go back.

The returning salmon has a dangerous journey ahead. It has to fight the river's powerful current, leaping and splashing up waterfalls, and avoid hungry bears. If it survives these dangers, the fish arrives back where it hatched with thousands of other salmon. Now the salmon can lay their eggs and breed. Sockeye salmon, exhausted, die after breeding. Their amazing journey is over, and the cycle starts again.

Parrot

A flash of bright color through the leaves of a rain forest tree may be a parrot. You'll know for sure when you hear its screeching calls. These birds fly around in noisy flocks, searching for ripe fruits to eat. Largest and noisiest of all are the macaws. A massive beak allows macaws to crack the toughest nuts, but also to gently peel fruits.

Macaws are among the world's smartest birds. Some even learn to copy human words! In a traditional myth of the Maya people of Mexico and Central America, there is a proud macaw god named Vucub-Caquix. The macaw tried to rule the world, until he was defeated by two heroic brothers.

Macaws eat mud! No one is sure why, but it might be a source of salt.

Blue and yellow macaw,
South America

Quokkas are very rare. To have the best chance of seeing one, you need to visit an island called Rottnest, west of Australia.

Quokka

Check out the grin on this quokka! No wonder people often call it the world's happiest animal. However, it is not really smiling—that's just how it looks to us. The quokka is a kind of mammal called a marsupial, like a kangaroo, but it is the size of a fat rabbit. Unlike kangaroos, however, quokkas are pretty good at climbing trees. Some Aboriginal people of Australia called this animal "gwaga." Later, that became quokka.

Quokkas eat mostly plants. After they swallow their food, they bring it back up and chew it a second time. Why? It probably helps them squeeze more nutrients from the tough leaves.

Quokka, Australia

Squirrel monkey

Squirrel monkeys make friends by taking turns cleaning each other's fur.

Common squirrel monkey, South America

Young squirrel monkeys love to play. Jumping, chasing one another, and pulling the tails of adults are some of their favorite games. Squirrel monkeys have the biggest brains for their size of all monkeys. Like humans, playing is how they learn. They usually live in groups of forty monkeys, but sometimes there are more than two hundred.

Squirrel monkeys chatter and twitter in the treetops, sounding like a flock of birds. When one finds juicy fruits or insects to eat, the rest of the group gathers around. To help others follow it, a squirrel monkey will wipe pee on its hands to leave a smelly trail behind.

Viscacha

South America's highest mountains are the kingdom of the viscacha. It has a body and ears like a rabbit, legs like a kangaroo, and a long tail like a squirrel, but its closest relative is actually the chinchilla. Its long back legs help it jump from rock to rock, and it can easily climb steep cliffs.

Up in the mountains, the air is chilly and fierce winds blow. To stay cozy, the viscacha has very thick fur. It also spends hours in the morning sitting in the sun with its eyes closed. Hundreds of years ago, the Inca people used to wear clothes made from this animal's soft fur.

Viscachas often roll around in the dust. This is a great way to get rid of bugs!

Spotted parrotfish,
Indian and western
Pacific Oceans

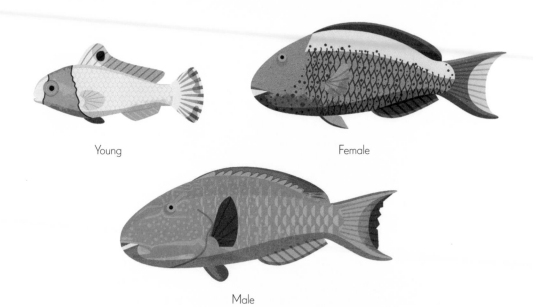

Young

Female

Male

Parrotfish

Crunch … crunch … crunch … Swim over a coral reef and you might hear parrotfish feeding. These noisy eaters munch on algae, which they scrape off rocks with their sharp beaks. The sound? As they remove the algae, the fish chomp into some of the crunchy coral at the same time. As it passes through the fish, it is broken down into sand—many white beaches are actually piles of parrotfish poop!

When the spotted parrotfish is young it is orange and white, but as it grows it becomes brown and turns into an adult female. It hasn't finished changing, though. As the female grows she becomes more colorful and turns into a male!

Some parrotfish make a sleeping bag out of slime to spend the night in!

Koala

You're most likely to find a koala snoozing in the fork of a tree. Koalas sleep or just sit for about twenty hours a day! Even when alert, they mostly just cling to trees and eat. Koalas are picky eaters. They only like the leaves of gum trees, also called eucalyptus. There isn't a lot of energy in a leafy diet, which is why koalas doze so much.

People often think koalas are bears, but they're not. They belong to a group of mammals called marsupials. A newborn koala is the size of a jelly bean and can't see or hear anything, so, like kangaroos, mother koalas carry their babies in a snug pouch on their belly.

Koala means "no drink" in one of the languages of the Aboriginal people of Australia. Eating leaves gives koalas most of the water they need.

Koala, eastern Australia

Owl

In the inky darkness of the night, owls go hunting. Their huge eyes can spot movement in the dimmest light. Owls can't move their eyes, so to look in different directions, they turn their whole head. They can twist it almost all the way around! Their keen ears are hidden below their feathers. The tufts that look like ears on owls like the eagle owl are actually just bundles of feathers.

Eagle owls are the largest of all owls. In a sudden, silent swoop, they grab prey as big as foxes and young deer. Super-soft edges to their feathers help them fly without a noise, and sharp, curved talons hold the meal tight as they carry it away.

In Ancient Greece, the goddess of wisdom, Athena, was often shown with an owl.

Sloth

High up in the rain forest is where sloths feel happiest. They edge through trees in slow motion, using their curved claws to grip the branches. Hooked on like this, they will hang around in the same tree for hours. They're not lazy, but it takes them a long time to digest their diet of leaves and twigs.

Three-toed sloths, such as the brown-throated sloth, have thick, shaggy fur. Tiny plantlike algae grow on their hair, turning it green, and it is even home to its own type of sloth moth. About once a week, sloths make the long journey all the way down to the bottom of the trees. Why? To go to the bathroom!

Sloths are surprisingly good swimmers.
They cross rivers doing a dog paddle.

Brown-throated sloth, Central and South America

The fennec fox is smaller than most pet cats,
and it weighs less, too.

Fox

In stories, foxes are often sneaky and play tricks. Real foxes are not like that, of course, although they do have amazing senses of smell and hearing. A fox can hear a mouse squeaking 100 ft (30 m) away!

The most common fox is the red fox, which you might see slinking down city streets after dark, but the smallest fox is the tiny fennec fox. It lives in deserts, where its pale fur camouflages it against the sand. Its delicate body is built to keep cool, with oversized ears to help it lose heat in the burning desert sun, and paws that are furry underneath to protect them from hot sand.

Arctic hare, Canada, Greenland, and the Arctic

Hare

Long back legs make hares great runners. They race across the ground at up to 47 mph (75 kph) to escape danger. The world's fastest human sprinters can reach only 28 mph (45 kph). To get a head start, hares also have big ears, which help them hear danger a long way off.

The Arctic hare lives in the frozen north, where there are no trees. It has a clever disappearing trick. In summer, it is brown or gray, but in winter, the hare turns white to match the snow and ice. Then its enemies can't see it. The hare's main predators are Arctic foxes and snowy owls—both of which also turn white in winter!

In the worst snowstorms, the Arctic hare digs a snow shelter to keep warm.

Kiwi

A kiwi is round, fat, and fluffy. You can't really see its wings, and it can't fly. In New Zealand, where kiwis live, the Maori people tell a story about how the kiwi lost its wings. The god of the forest asked all the birds to come down from the sky and eat the bugs that were attacking the trees. The only bird to agree to give up its wings and help was the kiwi.

Kiwis hunt at night. Their eyesight is poor, so they find creepy-crawlies to eat by smell and feel. Unusually, a kiwi's nostrils are at the tip of its bill, which it keeps poking into the earth as it walks to sniff out food.

Kiwis may seem shy, but they aren't pushovers.
They can kick and slash with their sharp claws.

Northern brown kiwi,
North Island of New Zealand

Each back leg of the male platypus has a
sharp, venomous claw. You don't want
a scratch from a platypus!

Platypus, eastern Australia

Platypus

The body of an otter, the beak and webbed feet of a duck, and the tail of a beaver—it could only be the platypus. When people outside of Australia saw it for the first time, many believed this peculiar mammal wasn't real.

The platypus uses its unusual rubbery beak like a scanner. It swishes the beak back and forth underwater, picking up tiny electrical signals coming from creatures hidden in the riverbed. Worms in mud? No problem. Shrimp under a rock? Easy. Instead of teeth, the adult platypus has hard pads in its beak to help grind up food. Even stranger, while mammals usually give birth to their babies, a female platypus lays eggs!

Panther chameleon, Madagascar

Chameleon

With the ability to change color, chameleons are some of the most magical members of the animal kingdom. They use different colors to send messages to each other, such as "I'm angry!," or to help control their temperature. Most chameleons live in forests and are expert climbers. They have feet that can grip tightly and a flexible tail that can wrap around branches as they move through the trees.

The chameleon's hidden secret is a long tongue like a catapult. When a chameleon fires it at an insect or spider, it stretches to hit the target. Smack! The sticky end holds the prey, then pulls it right back into the chameleon's mouth.

A chameleon can't match every background, but some chameleons change color to help hide themselves in their natural surroundings.

Gila monster

You may not think that monsters exist, but there is one lurking in the sandy deserts of Mexico and the USA. There's no need to worry, though, because the Gila (hee-luh) monster is actually a lizard. Its skin is covered with what look like shiny, colorful beads, but these are bony scales that protect it from bites.

The Gila sticks its tongue out to taste the air for food. Small animals and bird eggs are its favorites. Luckily for its prey, the Gila stores fat in its tail, a bit like a camel storing fat in its hump. This means it may only need to eat five or six times a year.

Gila monster,
Mexico and
southern US

The Gila monster has a venomous bite that can be really painful, but it is not usually strong enough to kill a human.

Meerkat

When meerkats sunbathe, they do it standing up. The dark fur around their eyes acts like sunglasses.

Meerkats are great team players. Their gang is called a mob and has as many as forty meerkats in it. Most end up on babysitting duty. The adults take turns being guards. The lookouts stand up on their back legs or climb a rock to get a better view.

Meerkats have their own special language. Each cheep, squeak, yelp, and bark is like a word. One kind of bark means there is danger in the sky—like a hawk or an eagle. Another bark says to watch out for a snake or wild dog on the ground. All the meerkats have different calls, so they can recognize their friends.

Meerkat, southern Africa

Piranha

River creatures watch out! A piranha's jaws are full of sharp, white teeth, and they snap shut with massive force. If a piranha were the same size as a T. rex, guess which would have the strongest bite? The piranha! These fierce and fast little fish lurk in South American rivers. To see who is fiercest, they have staring contests.

The red-bellied piranha has a taste for other fish. It bites off chunks of flesh or gobbles down smaller prey whole. However, other kinds of piranha aren't as bloodthirsty. As well as meat, they will chomp on plants and forest fruits that plop into their river.

Piranhas bark like dogs. The strange sound doesn't come from their mouth, but from deep inside their belly.

Red-bellied piranha,
South America

Keel-billed toucan,
Central America

When toucans go to
sleep, they twist their
head around to rest their
huge beak on their back.

Toucan

It's easy to see why the Aztec people thought that a toucan's beak was made from rainbows. The colorful bill is so enormous you wonder how this beautiful bird can move. In fact, the beak has thin sides and is filled with air spaces, so it is actually very light. Its sharp edges are perfect for snipping off fruits from forest trees. Swallowing is tricky, though—the toucan has to become a jungle juggler by tossing the food up in the air, then quickly opening wide to catch it. Gulp! Toucans live in small flocks and call to one another with loud, frog-like croaks as they hop from tree to tree.

Tortoise

Tortoises are the tanks of the animal world. They're slow and clumsy, but these reptiles have no need to go fast. Their thick shell is a heavy shield. If anything tries to attack a tortoise, it just pulls its head and legs in, peeking out until the coast is clear. In fact, many stories across the world have the wise, plodding tortoise competing against the playful, speedy hare—and winning!

Red-footed tortoises live in South America and grow to 20 in (50 cm), but on some islands there are giant tortoises that weigh as much as a tiger. The Hindu religion has a story about an even bigger tortoise that carries the whole world on its shell.

Tortoises are ancient animals. The first tortoises were alive 200 million years ago, when dinosaurs ruled the Earth.

Red-footed tortoise, South America

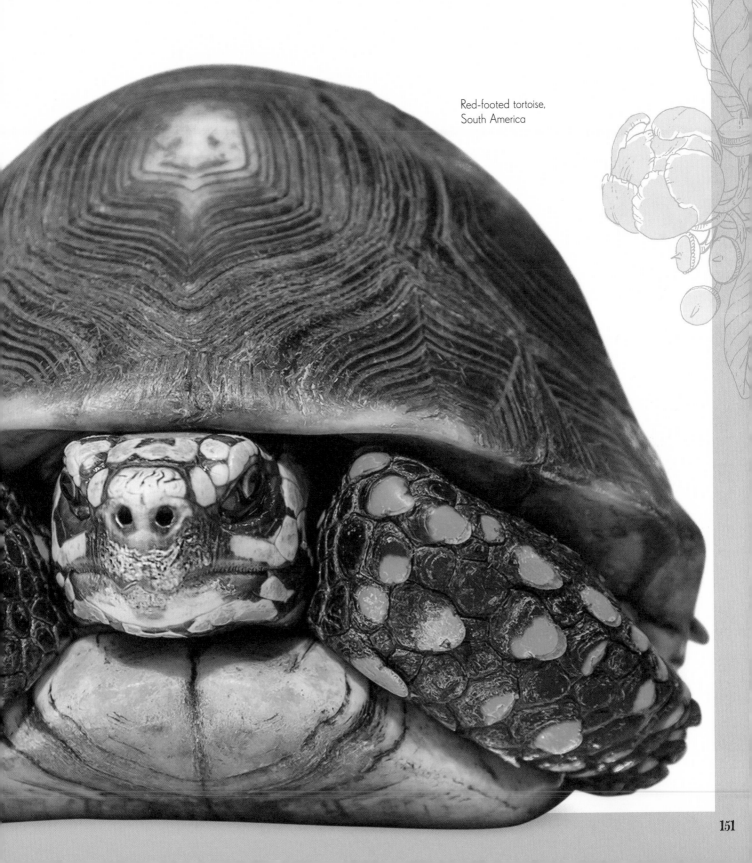

Caecilian

Y ou would be forgiven for thinking this was an earthworm, but a jaw full of curved teeth makes this a caecilian (suh-sill-yun). They are amphibians, like frogs and newts. Few people see these weird animals because they are found either burrowing below the soil or swimming around like wiggly eels.

Caecilians don't have arms or legs. They can't see very well—some have no eyes—and they feel and smell their way around. Some caecilians lay eggs, but others, such as the Veragua caecilian, give birth to miniature versions of themselves. A few mother caecilians offer their babies a very strange treat: their own skin! The babies nibble bits off, then wait for it to regrow.

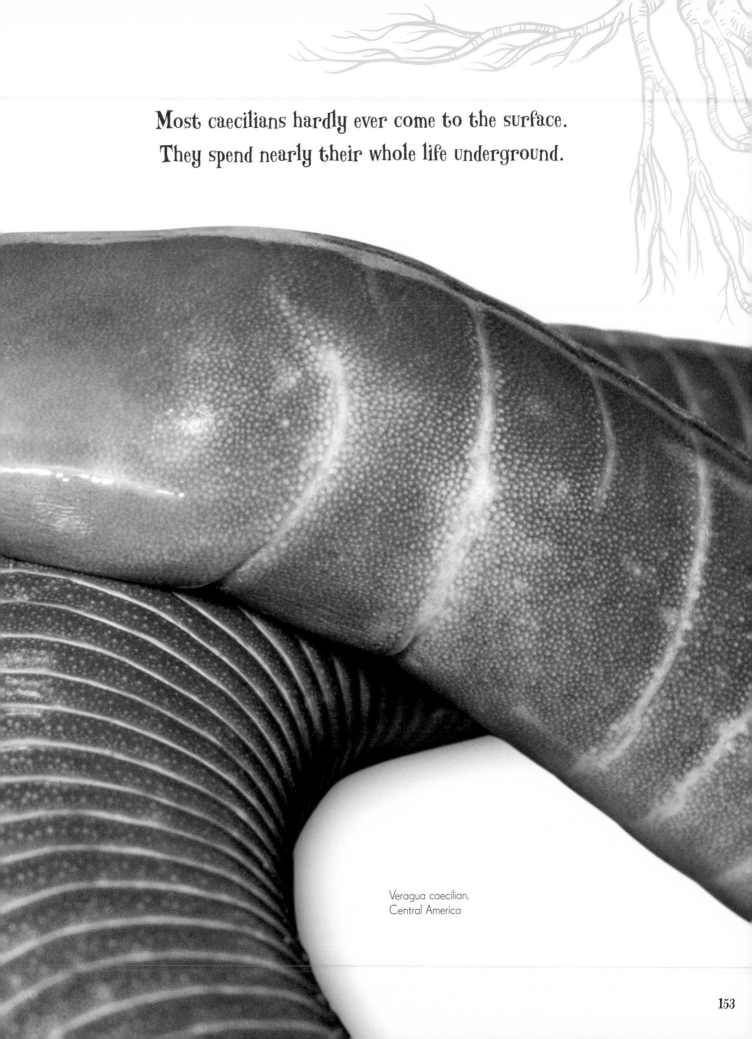

Most caecilians hardly ever come to the surface.
They spend nearly their whole life underground.

Veragua caecilian,
Central America

Flying fish

Everyone knows fish can't fly, but that's actually not quite true. If you're lucky, in some parts of the world you might see flying fish skimming just above the waves, their silvery blue bodies glittering in the sun. They wiggle their tail quickly to propel themselves into the air and then open their winglike fins to glide. They don't do this for fun, but to escape danger below the surface, such as being chased by hungry dolphins.

The Tao people of Orchid Island in the Pacific Ocean have festivals dedicated to these incredible fish. Their calendar even has three seasons—one for when the flying fish arrive, one for when they leave, and one for when there are no fish at all.

Flying fish can glide farther than the length of three and half football fields before splashing back into the sea.

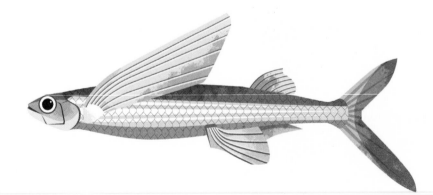

Bennett's flying fish,
worldwide tropical oceans

Common flying gecko,
Southeast Asia

Common leopard gecko,
southern Asia

Gecko

What's that looking at you from the ceiling? Is it a gecko? Many geckos come out to hunt for insects after the sun goes down. Pads on their feet give incredible grip. Millions of tiny hairs on the pads cling to almost any surface, so geckos can scoot up slippery glass or shiny metal easily. They can even run across a ceiling upside down. Scientists study gecko feet to create new materials, such as a super-sticky fabric that lets people climb up walls!

Most geckos are colorful, but some have patterns just like tree bark to help them hide. They croak and chirp through the night. The tokay gecko cries "To—kay!," which is how it got its name.

Electric blue gecko, Tanzania

Most geckos don't have eyelids. They lick their huge eyes to keep them clean and wet.

Madagascar day gecko, Madagascar

Tokay gecko, southern Asia and Southeast Asia

Frilled leaf-tail gecko, Madagascar

Leafy seadragon,
Australia

Seadragon

Seadragons are some of the strangest fish in the sea. The leafy seadragon in particular looks more like seaweed than a fish. It has flaps of skin that make wavy branches, helping to disguise it. The seadragon also drifts along like seaweed, so that a predator might swim straight by and not recognize it. For a mouth, seadragons have a tube that is perfect for sucking up shrimp and tiny plankton.

Seadragons are cousins of seahorses. Like seahorses, it's the fathers that are in charge of the eggs. Each dragon dad carries around two hundred of them, which the female seadragon gives him. The eggs stick safely under his leafy tail until they are ready to hatch.

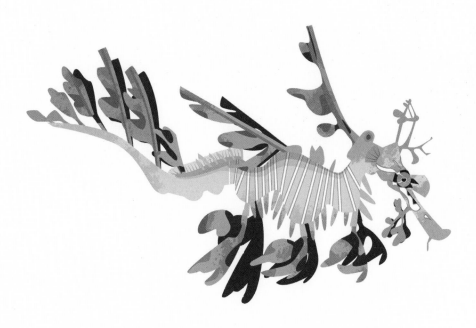

The male leafy seadragon's tail turns yellow
when he is ready to carry eggs.

Atlantic puffin,
North Atlantic Ocean

Puffin

In winter, the colorful parts of a puffin's beak
fall off, leaving it dull and gray.

With their colorful beak and bright-orange feet, puffins look
pretty fancy. On land they walk with a funny waddle, and
because of this and their bright colors they are sometimes called
"clowns of the sea." When they're annoyed with each other, grumpy
puffins stomp around with their beaks open.

All winter, Atlantic puffins have to face storms and mighty waves.
When spring comes at last, they return to cliffs to nest. Puffin parents
dig a hole or reuse a rabbit burrow where they raise their one chick,
called a puffling. This hungry fluffball will grow fatter than its parents.
They bring it lots of shiny fish, lined up neatly in their beaks.

The teeth of the viperfish are see-through,
which makes them almost invisible to prey.

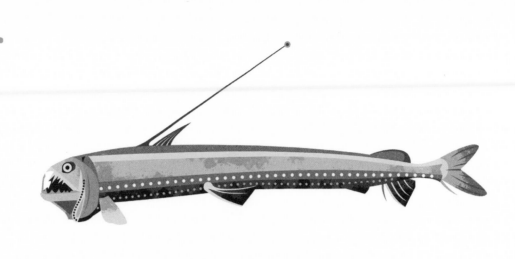

Viperfish

In the deeper parts of the ocean the water is as dark as night. Here in the gloomy, cold waters you will find some of the scariest-looking fish, including the frightening viperfish. It is also called the fangfish because of its huge teeth.

The viperfish is a fierce hunter. As well as huge eyes to help it see, it has its own flashlight—a light at the end of a long spine on its back. The viperfish flashes this on and off to attract food such as shrimp and smaller fish. In the darkness they swim closer until it's too late—gulp! The viperfish's jaws can open extra wide to swallow prey whole.

Sloane's viperfish, worldwide

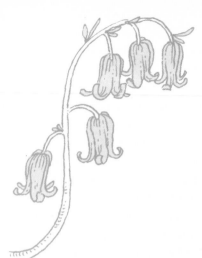

You might not believe it,
but hedgehogs can climb trees.

Hedgehog

Spines cover a hedgehog from head to tail. They are actually special spiky hairs and, if you get too close, the hedgehog rolls into a prickly ball to stay safe. Baby hedgehogs are born naked, but after only a few hours spines start popping out all over their pink-and-gray skin.

The European hedgehog wakes up after dark to rustle around looking for creepy-crawlies to munch. In winter, it falls into a deep sleep called hibernation. It might nap for five months, so you wouldn't want to invite it to a sleepover! While it hibernates, its body chills to 43°F (6°C), which is only a little warmer than the inside of a fridge.

Starfish

Starfish are topsy-turvy animals. Their eyes are at the end of their arms. Their mouth is underneath where their bottom should be, and their bottom is on top where their head should be. In fact, they don't even have a head. Somehow they move around without a brain or heart, and instead of blood, they are full of seawater.

Under each of a starfish's arms are hundreds of sticky feet. They grab prey and carry it to the mouth. The starfish then pushes its stretchy stomach out of its body, digests the meal, and sucks it back in! Amazingly, if a starfish loses an arm, it grows back—some starfish can regrow their whole body from just one arm.

Red cushion star, western Atlantic Ocean and Caribbean Sea

Red spine star, Indian and Pacific Oceans

Blue starfish, Indian
and Pacific Oceans

Granulated starfish,
Indian and Pacific Oceans

Most starfish have five arms.
Some have ten, twenty, or even fifty!

Common starfish,
northern Atlantic Ocean

Crown-of-thorns starfish,
Indian and Pacific Oceans

Necklace starfish,
Indian and
Pacific Oceans

Common sunstar, northern
Atlantic and Pacific Oceans

Axolotl

You are looking at one of the strangest animals on Earth. It's called an axolotl (ak-suh-lot-uhl). The name comes from an old Aztec word meaning "water servant." If you think it looks like a weird tadpole, that's because it is. Like frogs, axolotls are amphibians, so they start life in water. But they never change into adults! The frilly things on each side of their head are gills, which they use to breathe.

Axolotls are rare in the wild. They only live in one lake near Mexico City, Mexico. If they get hurt, they have an amazing superpower—they can grow new body parts. They can even replace a leg, eye, lung, tail, or part of a heart!

In tanks, you often see pale-pink axolotls. However, in the wild, most are gray, green, or black.

Axolotl,
Mexico

Mother slow lorises lick venomous spit onto their babies to keep them safe. No one will touch them now.

Slow loris

Enormous eyes give you a clue to how the slow loris lives. Like an owl, it needs them to see in the dark. As night falls, it goes off to explore. The loris is a very slow animal. It takes its time with every move it makes. This helps it save energy. Being slow does not mean the loris is weak, though. A bite from a loris can give you a rash and burn your skin. It makes an oil near its elbows, which, when mixed with spit, creates venom.

Sadly, many slow lorises are caught to be sold as pets. However, though they look cute, they don't make good companions. The best place for lorises is the rain forest.

Toad

Toads try to look bigger to scare off predators by inflating their lungs to puff themselves up.

A chorus of croaking coming from a pond at night will show you the way to a group of toads or frogs. You can tell a toad from a frog by a toad's rough, warty skin. In European stories, toads are often used by witches in their spells, but in ancient Chinese tales, toads can be magicians themselves.

The largest toad is the cane toad from South America. Its appetite is enormous. In the 1930s, thousands were shipped to Australia to eat beetle pests. Unfortunately, they spread, and now there are millions of cane toads in Australia. They make a milky poison from their neck, which kills animals that eat them. Now the toads are the pests!

Cane toad, Central and
South America

Like many moths, the comet moth never feeds.
It does all of its eating as a caterpillar.

Comet moth,
Madagascar

Moth

If you leave a light on when you go to bed, you might find a moth fluttering around it. Some people think the moth confuses the bright glow of the bulb with the moon. Most moths fly at night and use the moon to guide them.

Moths have many ways to avoid being eaten. Some pretend to be dead leaves or bird poop. The comet moth has two long tails, each about the length of a pencil, which attackers target instead of the moth's body. It is one of the largest moths in the world, but it only lives for a few days. The males use their bushy antennae to smell out a female before their time runs out.

Mole

To sniff prey underwater, the star-nosed mole
blows bubbles then sucks them back up
its nose to smell what's nearby!

Star-nosed mole,
eastern North America

Moles spend nearly all their life underground, and they are digging machines. Their hands are curved into shovels— great for scooping out earth to make long tunnels. They pop up onto the surface sometimes, pushing soil onto the ground and making volcano-shaped molehills.

Moles' eyes are so tiny, they can barely see. They feel their way along their dark tunnels using their nose and whiskers. Juicy earthworms are what they're after. The star-nosed mole has twenty-two little pink arms around its nose, which it uses to sniff out food. It hunts in water as well as soil, and gobbles a meal in 0.2 seconds. That's faster than any other mammal!

Hummingbird

Red, orange, yellow, green, blue, indigo, and violet ... hummingbirds come in many beautiful colors. Species like the violet-tailed sylph also have beautiful long tails. Hummingbirds fly so fast, they whiz past in a blur. Their little wings can beat up to two hundred times a second, making the humming noise that gives them their name. Like helicopters, they can hover and even fly backward!

Most hummingbirds live in the forests of Central and South America. Because they fly so fast, they are always hungry and they drink flower nectar to build up their energy. They need to visit one to two thousand blooms every day. The Portuguese name for hummingbirds means "flower kissers."

Violet-tailed sylph, South America

Hummingbirds take about 250 breaths
a minute to help power their super-fast wings.

Scorpion

What's that hiding in the shadows? Yikes! It's a scorpion. Related to spiders, these terrifying-looking creatures have powerful pincers and a flexible tail tipped with a venomous sting. Quick as a flash, they can flick this over their head to defend themselves from hungry predators. One of the largest scorpions is the emperor scorpion, which can grow up to 8 in (20 cm) long. Most scorpions grab insects to eat, but even mice and lizards have to watch out when the emperor scorpion is around.

Many scorpions live in rain forests, but some live in deserts. These tough scorpions may never drink and can go a full year between meals.

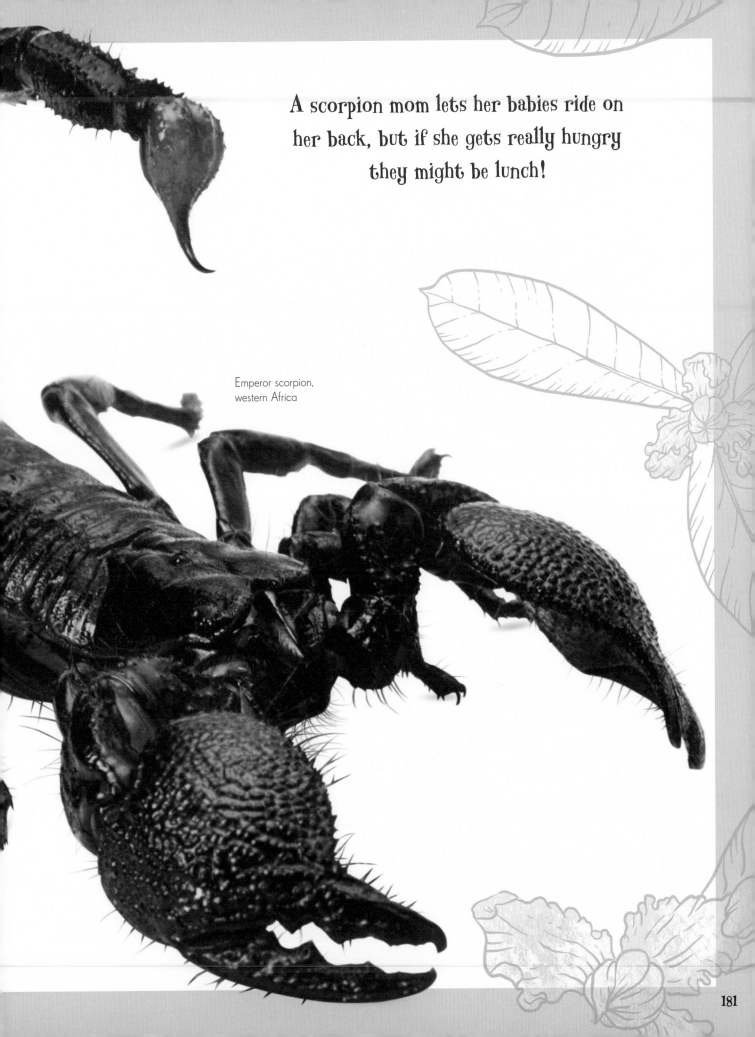

A scorpion mom lets her babies ride on her back, but if she gets really hungry they might be lunch!

Emperor scorpion, western Africa

Peacock mantis shrimp,
Indian and Pacific Oceans

Mantis shrimp

Mantis shrimp can see ultraviolet light,
which is what causes sunburn.

Mantis shrimp are definitely not wimps. The peacock mantis shrimp has a pair of deadly clubs on the ends of its front legs, which it holds tucked under its head, ready and waiting. When a crab or other shellfish comes near, the shrimp attacks as fast as a bullet, smashing open its prey's shell. Its punch is so quick, the water around its club boils and it even releases light!

This colorful creature has another secret weapon—its super eyesight. Its two eyes are packed with special sensors. Each eye can quickly figure out exactly how far away its dinner is. Humans have to use both eyes to do the same thing.

Butterfly

Glasswing butterflies have see-through wings.
If one landed here, you could read this
text right through it!

Common blue morpho,
Central and South America

A butterfly's wings are made of thousands of tiny flakes called scales. These overlap like the tiles on a roof and can be any color of the rainbow. The common blue morpho is nearly the size of a dinner plate, and it flashes in the sunlight like a jewel.

For mouths, butterflies have long drinking tubes to sip sweet nectar from flowers. However, most of these insects don't live long—perhaps only a few days or weeks. Many lay eggs, then die. Each egg hatches into a wormlike caterpillar, which eats and eats to grow fatter. Finally, it makes itself a hard case called a chrysalis. Safe inside, it rebuilds its body and comes out as a beautiful adult butterfly.

185

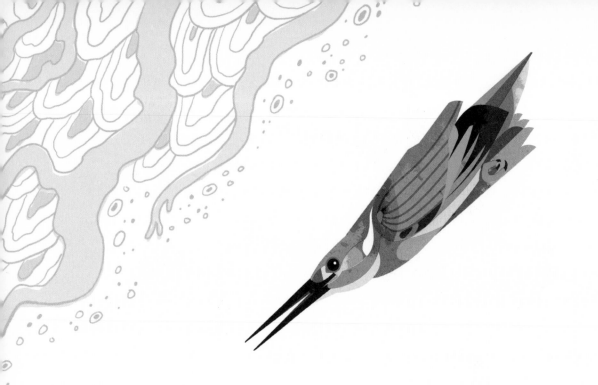

Kingfisher

All you will see when the common kingfisher speeds past is a blur of blue. To catch fish, the kingfisher waits on a branch, watching. Its amazing eyes can see under the shiny surface of the water. Suddenly, it dives. A second or two later, it's back on its branch with a fish in its beak. It swallows its fish head first, so the spines and scales slip down easily.

In Ancient Greece, it was said that kingfishers built nests that floated on the sea like magic, but really these birds dig burrows in riverbanks to raise their chicks in. The floor of their tunnel ends up carpeted in fishbones!

Not all kingfishers go near water. Many live in tropical forests and eat frogs, lizards, and insects, not fish.

Common kingfisher,
northern Africa,
Europe, and Asia

Sea slug

They may look like aliens from another planet, but sea slugs live in the ocean. Like their cousins that you can find in a garden, these slugs have soft, squishy bodies with no shell. They glide across the seabed on their slimy foot, squeezing into tiny gaps on coral reefs.

With their colorful skin and weird horns, sea slugs, such as the variable neon slug, look like they are headed to a costume party. Even the branching gills on their back are multicolored. Yet their bright colors are sending a message: "do not touch!" The skin of some sea slugs contains poison strong enough to kill crabs and fish.

Sea slugs are both female and male at the same time.
This means that they can all lay eggs.

Variable neon slug,
Indian and Pacific Oceans

Clownfish talk to each other with chirps,
clicks, and pops. They make some of
these sounds with their teeth.

Clownfish

Clownfish live on coral reefs, the most colorful habitat in the sea.
If you want to see one of these fish, you need to look for a
sea anemone first. An anemone looks a bit like a plant, but it is an
animal, too, with many fingerlike tentacles. It loves having clownfish
around, because the fish clean it and fan fresh water over it. It even
feeds on clownfish poop! However, the clownfish don't work for free.
In return for their help, the anemone protects its fish friends from
bigger fish. Anemone tentacles have painful stingers that most fish
don't like to touch. Clownfish are covered in thicker slime than
other kinds of fish, though, and can safely snuggle among the
stings without being hurt.

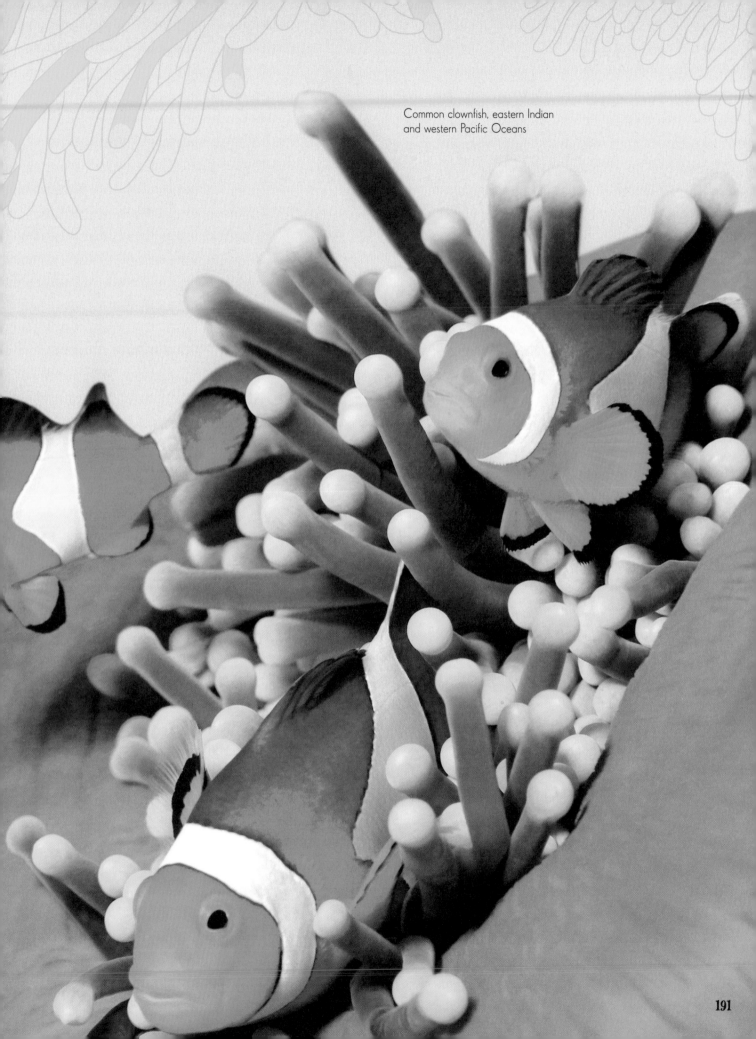

Common clownfish, eastern Indian and western Pacific Oceans

Dragonfly

Dragonfly-like insects first took to the skies 300 million years ago, which means they were on Earth long before birds or dinosaurs. These super-fast fliers have four wings that can each move in a different direction, enabling them to hover, fly upside down, and even travel backward. You will usually find them hanging still in the air above a pond, before zipping off to a new spot.

A dragonfly's favorite food is other insects. It spots them using its huge eyes, which lock onto their target while they chase it. With nine out of every ten attacks ending in a kill, dragonflies are some of the best predators in the animal kingdom.

Dragonflies lay their eggs in water, and their fierce larvae prey on tadpoles and beetles.

Southern migrant hawker, northern Africa, southern Europe, and Asia

Egg

Tadpole

Froglet

Adult frog

Frog

An ugly frog turns into a handsome prince in the fairy tale, but this is unfair! Frogs come in all sorts of amazing shapes and colors, and can be very pretty. Poison dart frogs can be multicolored, and mossy frogs have stunning camouflage. Their bumpy skin helps them pretend that they are clumps of green moss.

Most kinds of frog grow up by a process called metamorphosis. They begin life as frogspawn—blobs inside a coat of jelly. Wriggling tadpoles hatch out and breathe underwater, using gills. Eventually they grow legs and become tiny froglets. Now they can start to breathe air. Finally, they lose their tail and become adults, ready to hop onto land!

Suckers on the mossy frog's toes
help it stick to slippery rocks.

Mossy frog,
Southeast Asia

You won't find a grasshopper's
ears on its head. They are hidden
behind its back legs.

Grasshopper

In the summer, grassy places buzz with insects. Many of them are grasshoppers. Male grasshoppers make a chirping song to attract a partner. They rub their back legs against their wings, like they are playing a violin. In Ancient China, people kept grasshoppers as musical pets.

Grasshopper jaws are made for chewing plants, and the insects can be pests. Normally they live on their own, but when certain types of grasshopper gather in big numbers they are known as locusts. When the desert locust joins a crowd, it changes completely. It turns from brown to bright yellow and gets a big appetite. These locusts create super-swarms containing billions of insects, which can eat whole fields of crops, leaving nothing behind but bare stalks.

Jeweled flower mantis, India and Southeast Asia

Praying mantis

A female mantis will eat a male if she gets the chance.
It gives her extra energy to lay eggs.

A praying mantis sits as still as a statue, with its front legs together. It looks as if it is praying, but really, it is waiting to prey on other insects. Its huge, curved claws are powerful weapons. In the blink of an eye, out they flick to grab any food in range. The mantis grips its victim using spikes as sharp as needles, then eats it alive. Amazing eyesight makes mantises extra-deadly. They are the only insects to see in 3-D like we do.

Many mantises are disguised to keep them safe from hungry predators. However, some mantises have a clever trick. If alarmed, they raise their arms and flash their colorful wings to warn attackers away.

In some male fiddler crabs the right claw is larger, and in others it is the left claw.

Crab

Crabs can walk, run, and swim ... but only sideways! A crab's legs are attached to the sides of its body, so it is usually easier for them to move left or right. Of a crab's ten legs, eight of them are used to get around, while the front two are pincers for holding and crushing food. Most crabs will eat almost anything, dead or alive.

With its one king-size claw a male fiddler crab looks like it means business. His claw can weigh over half his body weight! He waves this giant claw at female crabs to show how strong he is, and also uses it as a weapon—any male who tries to steal his seaside burrow is likely to receive a mighty snap!

Atlantic marsh fiddler crab, eastern North America

Beetle

The Ancient Egyptians thought that the dung beetle god, Khepri, rolled the sun across the sky.

Large green dung beetle, Africa

Ýou may think that large animals rule the land, but really beetles do. There are huge numbers of these tough insects and they live almost everywhere, from seashores to mountaintops. The only place without beetles is the ocean.

Think of a type of food, and there's a beetle that eats it. With their strong jaws, beetles feed on plants, roots, wood, animals, and rotting things. Some even eat each other. Dung beetles reuse poop left by bigger animals. They roll it into little balls, which they bury for their young, called grubs, to feast on. Some dung beetles are thieves, though! They steal poop balls from each other instead of making their own.

Leafcutter ant,
Central and
South America

Ant

On its own, one ant is not very powerful, but ants in a group behave like a single strong animal. An ant mega-group is called a colony and is ruled by a queen. She is served by thousands of daughters, called workers, and protected by soldiers, who guard the colony, often with huge jaws and painful stings.

Ants eat lots of different foods. Army ants march through forests catching unlucky creepy-crawlies, and honeypot ants swell up as they store sweet nectar from flowers in their belly—people in Australia and North America used to suck them like candy! Leafcutter ants are farmers. The workers cut leaves and carry them to their nest. Here the leaves rot, and fungi grow on them. The ants then eat the fungi.

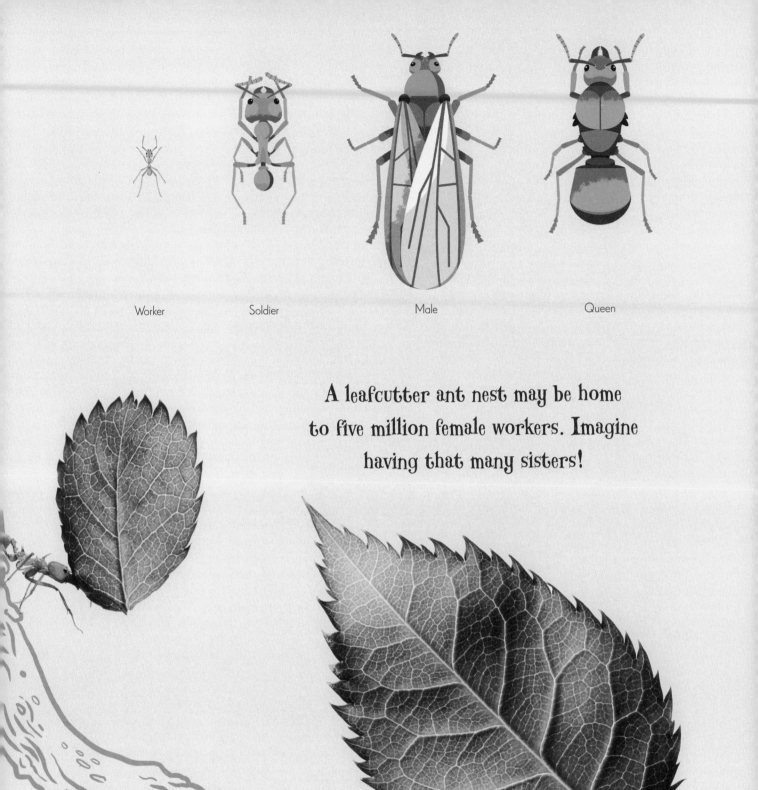

Worker Soldier Male Queen

A leafcutter ant nest may be home
to five million female workers. Imagine
having that many sisters!

Bug

So far we have found 80,000 species of bug. Every year we keep finding new ones. Not all insects are bugs. To be bugs, they have to have a sharp beak to suck up food with. Many are vegetarian, but others are deadly hunters.

Bugs are an amazing bunch. Cicadas are so noisy they keep people awake at night. Pond skaters can walk on the surface of water. Froghoppers jump more than one hundred times their body length, and stink bugs fire smelly bombs at their enemies. Thorn bugs pretend to be sharp thorns. This clever camouflage works best when they gather on a branch, so they can safely poke their mouths into the plant to drink the sap inside.

Thorn bugs have ants that guard them. In return, they make a sweet liquid called honeydew for the ants.

Thorn bug, North, Central, and South America

Only female wasps can sting—male wasps do not have a stinger.

Cuckoo wasp, Europe

Wasp

A wasp sting is a painful lesson, so we quickly learn not to make them angry. A wasp's sharp stinger injects venom, making our skin itch and burn. Some have black and yellow stripes to warn attackers away, but wasps usually only sting for defense or to kill prey.

Tiny cuckoo wasps are less than 0.4 in (1 cm) long, and their body shines with metallic colors. Their young are parasites— they feed on other living insects. If you zoom in, you can see that the wasps are covered with dimples. These pits protect them from the stings of other insects, which are trying to protect their young from the wasps.

Two of the peacock spider's eight eyes are
so massive, they take up half its head.

Spider

If you had to design the ultimate hunter, you might give it eight
eyes, eight legs, and two sharp fangs. This is exactly what a
spider has. It uses its fangs to stab prey, injecting venom that stops it
from moving. Next the spider wraps it in threads of sticky silk, ready
to eat later, like a gruesome packed lunch. Don't worry, though—
only a few spiders are dangerous to humans.

The male of the tiny peacock spider is brightly colored, and is also a
great dancer. As if moving to music, he waves two legs in the air and
jumps around so his colors sparkle. If he's lucky, the female likes his
dance. If not, she might eat him!

Tree of life

We have named over a million species of animal, but there are probably millions more waiting to be found. All animals belong to the tree of life, which is an illustration showing how they are related to one another. Animals on branches closer together are more closely related. The groups that have lived on Earth the longest form the tree's lowest branches.

Carnivores

Odd-toed hoofed mammals

Primates

Rabbits

Pangolins

Reptiles

If it has tough, dry skin covered in scales then it's a reptile. These animals' bodies do not make heat, so to warm up they often sunbathe. Most lay eggs, which can have a hard or soft shell.

Rodents

Marsupials

Lizards and snakes

Turtles and tortoises

Crocodiles

Birds

Fish

These amazing animals can all breathe underwater. Some live in the salty sea and others in freshwater. Usually fish have smooth scales, but sharks and rays have small, rough scales that feel like sandpaper.

Bony fish

Birds

Swooping through the skies, or running along the ground, you can tell a bird by its feathers and hard beak. Birds are descended from dinosaurs, and just like these ancient reptiles they lay hard-shelled eggs.

Sharks

Starfish

Jellyfish

Rays

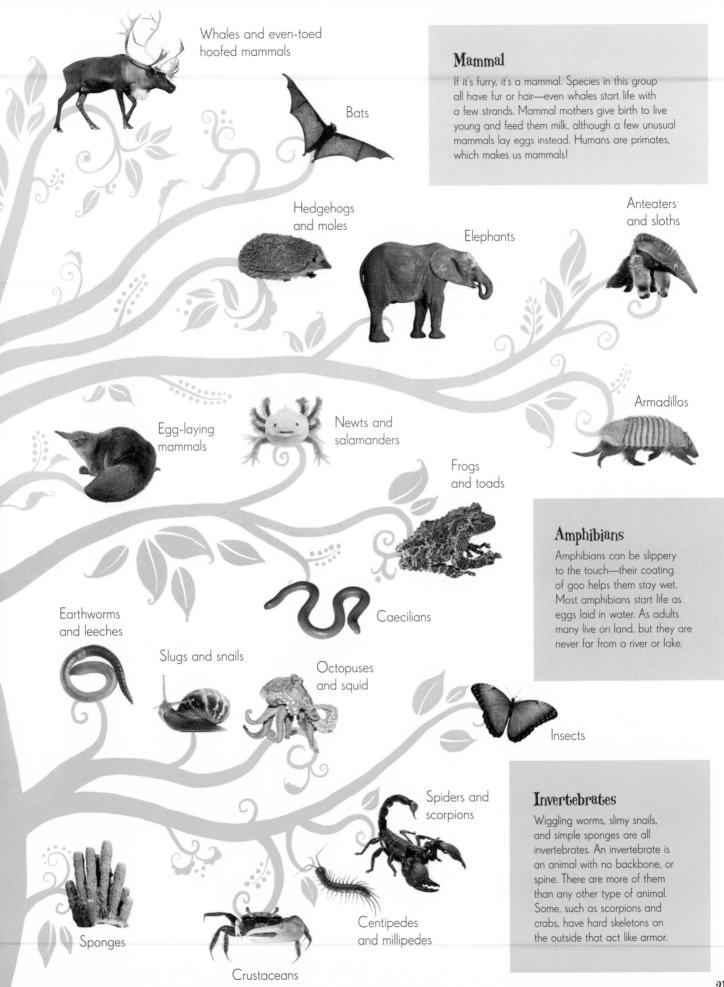

Whales and even-toed hoofed mammals

Bats

Mammal

If it's furry, it's a mammal. Species in this group all have fur or hair—even whales start life with a few strands. Mammal mothers give birth to live young and feed them milk, although a few unusual mammals lay eggs instead. Humans are primates, which makes us mammals!

Hedgehogs and moles

Elephants

Anteaters and sloths

Armadillos

Egg-laying mammals

Newts and salamanders

Frogs and toads

Amphibians

Amphibians can be slippery to the touch—their coating of goo helps them stay wet. Most amphibians start life as eggs laid in water. As adults many live on land, but they are never far from a river or lake.

Earthworms and leeches

Caecilians

Slugs and snails

Octopuses and squid

Insects

Spiders and scorpions

Invertebrates

Wiggling worms, slimy snails, and simple sponges are all invertebrates. An invertebrate is an animal with no backbone, or spine. There are more of them than any other type of animal. Some, such as scorpions and crabs, have hard skeletons on the outside that act like armor.

Sponges

Centipedes and millipedes

Crustaceans

Glossary

algae Simple, plantlike life-forms mostly found in water, including the ocean. They can be tiny and too small for us to see, or very large, such as seaweeds

amphibian Animal with a backbone that usually spends part of its life in water and the rest on land. It usually develops from an egg to a larva, and then into an adult. Frogs and newts are examples of amphibians

antennae Sensitive feelers on the head of an insect, usually in pairs. Insects use their antennae to feel, smell, and taste the world around them

antlers Horn-like bones that grow on a deer's head

apes Group of mammals with big brains that are very clever with their hands, including gorillas and orangutans

bird Animal with a backbone that has a hard beak and feathers. Most birds can fly, and all lay hard-shelled eggs for which they often make a nest

blowhole Hole on the top of the head through which whales and dolphins breathe

blubber Thick layer of fat under the skin of some animals, such as penguins, seals, and whales. It keeps them warm in very cold habitats

camouflage Color or pattern that disguises an animal where it lives, to help it hide from attackers

captivity When an animal is kept by humans in a cage or zoo and is not living in the wild

carcass Dead body of an animal

coral reef Habitat found mainly in warm shallow seas. It is made from the rock-hard skeletons of billions of tiny animals called corals

desert Habitat found where there is very little rainfall. Deserts are usually sandy, and can be hot or cold

domestic animal Animal that is bred to be kept by humans, either for meat, wool, and to do work, or as a pet

echolocation Using sound to determine how far away an object is by listening for the echo from a call. Dolphins and some bats use echolocation to find their way around

endangered When an animal becomes very rare in the wild. If we do not do something to help, the animal might disappear forever and go extinct

excavate Dig up

extinct When the last member of a species dies and there are no more of its kind left anywhere on Earth

fish Animal with a backbone that usually spends its whole life in water and breathes using gills. Many fish have a bony skeleton, but fish such as sharks and rays have flexible skeletons made from a material called cartilage

fungi Life-forms, such as molds and mushrooms, that usually feed on rotting food

gills Organs used to breathe underwater. Fish and some amphibians have gills

habitat Place where animals, plants, and other living things are found. Habitats can be on land or in water. Many species live only in particular types of habitat

herbivore Animal that eats only plants

hibernation Deep sleep that some animals fall into over winter. It can last for many months

insect Animal with three pairs of legs and a body in three sections. These are the head, the thorax (in the middle), and the abdomen (at the back). Many insects also have two pairs of wings

invertebrate Animal with no backbone such as insects, spiders, crabs, and starfish

larvae Young of certain animals such as insects, amphibians, and jellyfish

legend Story from a long time ago that may or may not be true

mammal Animal with a backbone that has warm blood and has fur or hair. Most mothers give birth to live babies and all feed them milk

mane Collar or strip of long fur around or on the head of an animal such as a lion or zebra

marsupial Type of mammal that gives birth to tiny, weak babies that often cannot see or hear. The babies usually grow up in a pouch on the mother's belly. Most marsupials live in Australia, but some live in North, Central, and South America

metamorphosis When an animal has a dramatic change in its shape when it grows older. For example, when tadpoles change into frogs, or when caterpillars change into butterflies

migration Long journey made by animals to find a new place to feed or raise their families. Many animals migrate every year between their summer and winter homes

myth Story or tale that isn't true

nectar Sweet, sugary liquid made by flowers. Insects and birds visit the flowers to drink the nectar

ocean Huge area of salt water. The Earth has five oceans: the Atlantic, Arctic, Indian, Pacific, and Southern, which are all connected

parasite Animal that lives on another animal, or inside its body, and causes the animal harm. It feeds on the animal and cannot live without it. Examples are mosquitoes and ticks

plankton Tiny living things that drift in oceans, lakes, and ponds, and which are often too small for us to see. They include algae and small animals, such as shrimp

poison Harmful substance made by an animal as a defense. Poison often stays in the skin, and an attacker is only poisoned if it tries to eat the poisonous animal

predator Animal that hunts another animal, called prey, for food

prey Animal that is hunted by a predator

rain forest Forest habitat where it is very wet and rains a lot. The largest rain forests are in the world's hot, tropical areas, and their trees can be very tall. They are home to huge numbers of different plants and animals

reptile Animal with a backbone that has tough skin, is covered in hard scales, and usually lays eggs. Reptiles include snakes, lizards, and turtles

rodent Type of mammal with a pair of long, sharp teeth in the top and bottom jaw. These teeth never stop growing, but keep wearing down as the animal uses them. Rodents include mice, rats, squirrels, and beavers

sap Sugary liquid produced by plants. It moves around inside the trunk and branches, a bit like blood in animals

savanna Habitat of wide, open grassland in a hot, tropical part of the world. It may have scattered trees. The largest savannas are in Africa and South America

shellfish Animal that has a hard outer shell and lives in the ocean, such as a crab or mussel

spawn Eggs laid by a fish or an amphibian, usually in water, with a jellylike coat

species Particular type of animal, plant, or other living thing. For example, the lion and cheetah are different species of cat. Members of the same species can breed together to produce young, but they usually cannot breed with other species

swamp Wetland habitat that is flooded with water

talons Long, sharp, curved claws that some predators use to kill their prey. Birds with talons include owls, eagles, hawks, and vultures

tame Being used to humans. Pets are tame animals

termite Type of small insect that looks much like an ant, and which lives in big groups called colonies. Each termite colony makes a large nest from earth or clay

tusk Long teeth of some animals, including walruses and elephants

vegetarian Animal that eats only plants

venom Harmful liquid made by an animal as a defense. Venom is different from poison, because it is delivered by stingers or a bite into an attacker's body

webbed Having skin between the fingers or toes

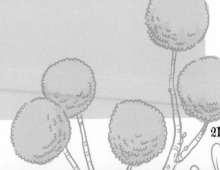

215

Visual guide

Humpback whale, page 4
Megaptera novaeangliae
Group: Mammal
Length: 56 ft (17 m)
Location: Worldwide

Orca, page 6
Orcinus orca
Group: Mammal
Length: 32 ft (9.8 m)
Location: Worldwide

African bush elephant, page 8
Loxodonta africana
Group: Mammal
Length with trunk and without tail: 25 ft (7.5 m)
Location: Africa

Saltwater crocodile, page 10
Crocodylus porosus
Group: Reptile
Length: 23 ft (7 m)
Location: Southeast Asia and Australia

Great hammerhead, page 12
Sphyrna mokarran
Group: Fish
Length: 20 ft (6.1 m)
Location: Worldwide

Giraffe, page 14
Giraffa camelopardalis
Group: Mammal
Height: 20 ft (6 m)
Location: Africa

White rhinoceros, page 16
Ceratotherium simum
Group: Mammal
Length with horn and without tail:
19 ft (5.7 m)
Location: Southern Africa

Common hippopotamus, page 18
Hippopotamus amphibius
Group: Mammal
Length without tail: 17 ft (5.1 m)
Location: Africa

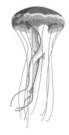

Pacific sea nettle, page 20
Chrysaora fuscescens
Group: Invertebrate
Tentacle length: 15 ft (4.6 m)
Location: Eastern Pacific Ocean

King cobra, page 22
Ophiophagus hannah
Group: Reptile
Length: 13 ft (4 m)
Location: Southeast Asia

Tiger, page 24
Panthera tigris
Group: Mammal
Length: 13 ft (4 m)
Location: Eastern Asia, southern Asia,
and Southeast Asia

Common bottlenose dolphin, page 26
Tursiops truncatus
Group: Mammal
Length: 12 ft (3.8 m)
Location: Worldwide

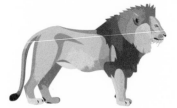

Lion, page 28
Panthera leo
Group: Mammal
Length: 11 ft (3.5 m)
Location: Africa and western India

Walrus, page 30
Odobenus rosmarus
Group: Mammal
Length: 11 ft (3.5 m)
Location: The Arctic

Indian peafowl, page 32
Pavo cristatus
Group: Bird
Length: 11 ft (3.5 m)
Location: Southern Asia

Dromedary camel, page 34
Camelus dromedarius
Group: Mammal
Length without tail: 11 ft (3.4 m)
Location: Northern Africa and the Arabian Peninsula

Moose, page 36
Alces alces
Group: Mammal
Length without tail: 10 ft (3 m)
Location: North America, Europe, and northern Asia

Swordfish, page 38
Xiphias gladius
Group: Fish
Length: 10 ft (3 m)
Location: Worldwide

Polar bear, page 40
Ursus maritimus
Group: Mammal
Length without tail: 9 ft (2.8 m)
Location: The Arctic

Common ostrich, page 42
Struthio camelus
Group: Bird
Height: 9 ft (2.8 m)
Location: Africa

Puma, page 44
Puma concolor
Group: Mammal
Length: 8 ft (2.5 m)
Location: North, Central, and South America

Plains zebra, page 46
Equus quagga
Group: Mammal
Length without tail: 8 ft (2.4 m)
Location: Eastern and southern Africa

Red kangaroo, page 48
Macropus rufus
Group: Mammal
Length: 8 ft (2.4 m)
Location: Australia

Snow leopard, page 50
Panthera uncia
Group: Mammal
Length: 8 ft (2.3 m)
Location: Central Asia

Emerald tree boa, page 52
Corallus caninus
Group: Reptile
Length: 7 ft (2.2 m)
Location: South America

Cheetah, page 54
Acinonyx jubatus
Group: Mammal
Length: 7 ft (2.2 m)
Location: Africa

Giant anteater, page 56
Myrmecophaga tridactyla
Group: Mammal
Length: 7 ft (2.1 m)
Location: Central and South America

Reindeer, page 58
Rangifer tarandus
Group: Mammal
Length without tail: 7 ft (2.1 m)
Location: North America, northern Europe,
and northern Asia

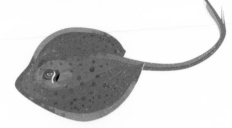

Blue-spotted ribbontail ray, page 60
Taeniura lymma
Group: Fish
Length: 7 ft (2 m)
Location: Indian and Pacific Oceans

African wild dog, page 62
Lycaon pictus
Group: Mammal
Length: 6 ft (1.8 m)
Location: Africa

Giant panda, page 64
Ailuropoda melanoleuca
Group: Mammal
Length without tail: 6 ft (1.8 m)
Location: China

Gray wolf, page 66
Canis lupus
Group: Mammal
Length: 6 ft (1.8 m)
Location: North America, Europe, Asia,
and the Arctic

Western gorilla, page 68
Gorilla gorilla
Group: Mammal
Height: 6 ft (1.8 m)
Location: Central Africa

Milk snake, page 70
Lampropeltis triangulum
Group: Reptile
Length: 6 ft (1.8 m)
Location: North, Central, and South America

Harp seal, page 72
Pagophilus groenlandicus
Group: Mammal
Length: 6 ft (1.7 m)
Location: Arctic Ocean

Bighorn sheep, page 74
Ovis canadensis
Group: Mammal
Length without tail: 6 ft (1.7 m)
Location: Western North America

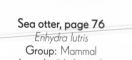

Sea otter, page 76
Enhydra lutris
Group: Mammal
Length: 5 ft (1.6 m)
Location: Northern Pacific Ocean

Marine iguana, page 78
Amblyrhynchus cristatus
Group: Reptile
Length: 5 ft (1.5 m)
Location: Galápagos Islands off South America

Bornean orangutan, page 80
Pongo pygmaeus
Group: Mammal
Height: 5 ft (1.4 m)
Location: Borneo in Southeast Asia

Wolverine, page 82
Gulo gulo
Group: Mammal
Length: 4 ft (1.3 m)
Location: North America, Europe, and Asia

Chilean flamingo, page 84
Phoenicopterus chilensis
Group: Bird
Height: 4 ft (1.3 m)
Location: South America

Common octopus, page 86
Octopus vulgaris
Group: Invertebrate
Length: 4 ft (1.3 m)
Location: Worldwide

Red panda, page 88
Ailurus fulgens
Group: Mammal
Length: 4 ft (1.2 m)
Location: Himalayan mountains and southwest China

American beaver, page 90
Castor canadensis
Group: Mammal
Length: 4 ft (1.2 m)
Location: North America

Green sea turtle, page 92
Chelonia mydas
Group: Reptile
Length: 4 ft (1.2 m)
Location: Tropical Atlantic, Pacific, and Indian Oceans

Golden pheasant, page 94
Chrysolophus pictus
Group: Bird
Length: 4 ft (1.2 m)
Location: China

Emperor penguin, page 96
Aptenodytes forsteri
Group: Bird
Height: 4 ft (1.2 m)
Location: Antarctica

Crested porcupine, page 98
Hystrix cristata
Group: Mammal
Length: 4 ft (1.1 m)
Location: Africa

Mandrill, page 100
Mandrillus sphinx
Group: Mammal
Length without tail: 4 ft (1.1 m)
Location: Central Africa

Ground pangolin, page 102
Smutsia temminckii
Group: Mammal
Length: 4 ft (1.1 m)
Location: Africa

Ring-tailed lemur, page 104
Lemur catta
Group: Mammal
Length: 4 ft (1.1 m)
Location: Madagascar

Rüppell's vulture, page 106
Gyps rueppelli
Group: Bird
Length: 3 ft (1 m)
Location: Northern and eastern Africa

Northern raccoon, page 108
Procyon lotor
Group: Mammal
Length: 3 ft (1 m)
Location: North and Central America

Lyle's flying fox, page 110
Pteropus lylei
Group: Mammal
Wingspan: 35 in (90 cm)
Location: Southeast Asia

Striped skunk, page 112
Mephitis mephitis
Group: Mammal
Length: 35 in (90 cm)
Location: North America

Sockeye salmon, page 114
Oncorhynchus nerka
Group: Fish
Length: 33 in (85 cm)
Location: Pacific Ocean

Blue and yellow macaw, page 116
Ara ararauna
Group: Bird
Length: 33 in (85 cm)
Location: South America

Quokka, page 118
Setonix brachyurus
Group: Mammal
Length: 33 in (85 cm)
Location: Australia

Common squirrel monkey, page 120
Saimiri sciureus
Group: Mammal
Length: 33 in (85 cm)
Location: South America

Common mountain viscacha, page 122
Lagidium viscacia
Group: Mammal
Length: 33 in (85 cm)
Location: Western South America

Spotted parrotfish, page 124
Cetoscarus ocellatus
Group: Fish
Length: 32 in (80 cm)
Location: Indian and western Pacific Oceans

Koala, page 126
Phascolarctos cinereus
Group: Mammal
Length: 32 in (80 cm)
Location: Eastern Australia

Eurasian eagle owl, page 128
Bubo bubo
Group: Bird
Length: 30 in (75 cm)
Location: Europe and Asia

Brown-throated sloth, page 130
Bradypus variegatus
Group: Mammal
Length: 28 in (70 cm)
Location: Central and South America

Fennec fox, page 132
Vulpes zerda
Group: Mammal
Length: 26 in (65 cm)
Location: Northern Africa

Arctic hare, page 134
Lepus arcticus
Group: Mammal
Length without tail: 26 in (65 cm)
Location: Canada, Greenland, and the Arctic

Northern brown kiwi, page 136
Apteryx mantelli
Group: Bird
Length: 26 in (65 cm)
Location: North Island of New Zealand

Platypus, page 138
Ornithorhynchus anatinus
Group: Mammal
Length: 26 in (65 cm)
Location: Eastern Australia

Panther chameleon, page 140
Furcifer pardalis
Group: Reptile
Length: 22 in (55 cm)
Location: Madagascar

Gila monster, page 142
Heloderma suspectum
Group: Reptile
Length: 22 in (55 cm)
Location: Mexico and southern USA

Meerkat, page 144
Suricata suricatta
Group: Mammal
Length: 22 in (55 cm)
Location: Southern Africa

Red-bellied piranha, page 146
Pygocentrus nattereri
Group: Fish
Length: 20 in (50 cm)
Location: South America

Keel-billed toucan, page 148
Ramphastos sulfuratus
Group: Bird
Length: 20 in (50 cm)
Location: Central America

Red-footed tortoise, page 150
Chelonoidis carbonarius
Group: Reptile
Length: 20 in (50 cm)
Location: South America

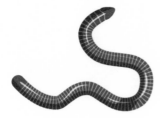

Veragua caecilian, page 152
Gymnopis multiplicata
Group: Amphibian
Length: 20 in (50 cm)
Location: Central America

Bennett's flying fish, page 154
Cheilopogon pinnatibarbatus
Group: Fish
Length: 16 in (40 cm)
Location: Worldwide tropical oceans

Tokay gecko, page 156
Gekko gecko
Group: Reptile
Length: 16 in (40 cm)
Location: Southern Asia and Southeast Asia

Leafy seadragon, page 158
Phycodurus eques
Group: Fish
Length: 14 in (35 cm)
Location: Australia

Atlantic puffin, page 160
Fratercula arctica
Group: Bird
Length: 14 in (35 cm)
Location: North Atlantic Ocean

Sloane's viperfish, page 162
Chauliodus sloani
Group: Fish
Length: 14 in (35 cm)
Location: Worldwide

European hedgehog, page 164
Erinaceus europaeus
Group: Mammal
Length without tail: 12 in (30 cm)
Location: Europe

Necklace starfish, page 166
Fromia monilis
Group: Invertebrate
Diameter: 12 in (30 cm)
Location: Indian and Pacific Oceans

Axolotl, page 168
Ambystoma mexicanum
Group: Amphibian
Length: 12 in (30 cm)
Location: Mexico

Javan slow loris, page 170
Nycticebus javanicus
Group: Mammal
Length: 10 in (25 cm)
Location: Java in Southeast Asia

Cane toad, page 172
Rhinella marina
Group: Amphibian
Length: 10 in (25 cm)
Location: Central and South America

Comet moth, page 174
Argema mittrei
Group: Invertebrate
Wingspan: 8 in (20 cm)
Location: Madagascar

Star-nosed mole, page 176
Condylura cristata
Group: Mammal
Length: 8 in (20 cm)
Location: Eastern North America

Violet-tailed sylph, page 178
Aglaiocercus coelestis
Group: Bird
Length: 8 in (20 cm)
Location: South America

Emperor scorpion, page 180
Pandinus imperator
Group: Invertebrate
Length: 8 in (20 cm)
Location: Western Africa

Peacock mantis shrimp, page 182
Odontodactylus scyllarus
Group: Invertebrate
Length: 7 in (18 cm)
Location: Indian and Pacific Oceans

Common blue morpho, page 184
Morpho peleides
Group: Invertebrate
Wingspan: 6 in (16 cm)
Location: Central and South America

Common kingfisher, page 186
Alcedo atthis
Group: Bird
Length: 6 in (16 cm)
Location: Northern Africa, Europe, and Asia

Variable neon slug, page 188
Nembrotha kubaryana
Group: Invertebrate
Length: 5 in (12 cm)
Location: Indian and Pacific Oceans

Common clownfish, page 190
Amphiprion ocellaris
Group: Fish
Length: 4 in (11 cm)
Location: Eastern Indian and western Pacific Oceans

Southern migrant hawker, page 192
Aeshna affinis
Group: Invertebrate
Wingspan: 3½ in (9 cm)
Location: Northern Africa, southern Europe, and Asia

Mossy frog, page 194
Theloderma corticale
Group: Amphibian
Length: 3½ in (9 cm)
Location: Southeast Asia

Desert locust, page 196
Schistocerca gregaria
Group: Invertebrate
Length: 3 in (7 cm)
Location: Africa and Asia

Jeweled flower mantis, page 198
Creobroter gemmatus
Group: Invertebrate
Length: 1½ in (4 cm)
Location: India and Southeast Asia

Atlantic marsh fiddler crab, page 200
Uca pugnax
Group: Invertebrate
Shell width: 1 in (2.3 cm)
Location: Eastern North America

Large green dung beetle, page 202
Garreta nitens
Group: Invertebrate
Length: ½ in (1.8 cm)
Location: Africa

Leafcutter ant, page 204
Atta cephalotes
Group: Invertebrate
Worker length: ½ in (1.4 cm)
Location: Central and South America

Thorn bug, page 206
Umbonia crassicornis
Group: Invertebrate
Length: ½ in (1 cm)
Location: North, Central, and South America

Cuckoo wasp, page 208
Holopyga generosa
Group: Invertebrate
Length: ¼ in (0.7 cm)
Location: Europe

Coastal peacock spider, page 210
Maratus speciosus
Group: Invertebrate
Length: ¼ in (0.4 cm)
Location: Australia

Editor Olivia Stanford
Project art editor Elle Ward
US editors Megan Douglass, Allison Singer
Additional editing Phil Hunt, Lizzie Davey
Additional design Hoa Luc, Jaileen Kaur
Jacket co-ordinator Francesca Young
Jacket designer Elle Ward
Senior pre-producer Nikoleta Parasaki
Pre-producer Nadine King
Producer Basia Ossowska
Picture research Sakshi Saluja
Senior DTP Designer Sachin Singh
DTP Designer Syed Mohd Farhan
Managing editor Laura Gilbert
Managing art editor Diane Peyton Jones
Delhi team head Malavika Talukder
Creative director Helen Senior
Publishing director Sarah Larter

Consultant Derek Harvey

First American edition, 2018
Published in the United States by DK Publishing
345 Hudson Street, New York, New York 10014

Copyright © 2018 Dorling Kindersley Limited
DK, a Divison of Penguin Random House LLC
18 19 20 21 22 10 9 8 7 6 5 4 3 2 1
001–309700–Oct/2018

A catalog record for this book
is available from the Library of Congress
ISBN: 978-1-4654-7702-6

DK books are available at special discounts when
purchased in bulk for sales promotions, premiums,
fund-raising, or educational use. For details, contact:
DK Publishing Special Markets, 345 Hudson Street,
New York, New York 10014
SpecialSales@dk.com

Printed and bound in China

A WORLD OF IDEAS:
SEE ALL THERE IS TO KNOW
www.dk.com

DK would like to thank: Gary Ombler for photography; Cotswold Wildlife Park and
Gardens for kindly allowing us to photograph their animals; Kathleen Teece for editorial
assistance; Fiona Macdonald, Emma Hobson, and Sonny Flynn for design assistance;
Jamie Ambrose for proofreading; Ishani Nandi, Anwesha Dutta, and Kritika Gupta for
picture research assistance; Daniel Long for the animal illustrations; Angela Rizza for the
pattern and foliage illustrations; Daniela Terrazzini for the cover illustration.

About the author: Ben Hoare has been fascinated by wildlife ever since he was a
toddler. He is the Features Editor of *BBC Wildlife Magazine* and has been an editor,
writer, or consultant for many DK books. His two daughters helped test this one.

Picture credits

The publisher would like to thank the following for their kind permission to reproduce their photographs:
(Key: a-above; b-below/bottom; c-center; f-far; l-left; r-right; t-top)

4-5 Alamy Stock Photo: WaterFrame. **6-7 Alamy Stock Photo:** Mauritius images GmbH. **8-9 Alamy Stock Photo:** Blickwinkel. **10-11 iStockphoto.com:** 35007. **12-13 Alamy Stock Photo:** Martin Strmiska. **14-15 Robert Harding Picture Library:** James Hager. **16 FLPA:** Tui De Roy / Minden Pictures. **18-19 Dreamstime.com:** Isselee. **20 Dreamstime.com:** Yiu Tung Lee. **22 Alamy Stock Photo:** Matthijs Kuijpers. **26-27 Getty Images:** Stephen Frink. **28 iStockphoto.com:** S. Greg Panosian. **30 Alamy Stock Photo:** RGB Ventures / SuperStock. **33 Fotolia:** Anekoho. **34-35 Alamy Stock Photo:** Stuart Forster. **36 naturepl.com:** Eric Baccega. **38-39 Alamy Stock Photo:** Paulo Oliveira. **40-41 FLPA:** Matthias Breiter / Minden Pictures. **42-43 iStockphoto. com:** Andrea Willmore. **45 Robert Harding Picture Library:** Frans Lanting. **46 Alamy Stock Photo:** Frans Lanting Studio. **48-49 Alamy Stock Photo:** imageBROKER. **50-51 Alamy Stock Photo:** Tierfotoagentur. **53 SuperStock:** Pete Oxford / Minden Pictures. **54-55 Getty Images:** Vittorio Ricci - Italy. **56-57 Alamy Stock Photo:** Life on White. **58-59 Alamy Stock Photo:** Ashley Cooper pics. **62-63 Alamy Stock Photo:** Uwe Skrzypczak. **65 Alamy Stock Photo:** Steve Bloom Images. **66-67 Alamy Stock Photo:** All Canada Photos. **68-69 Alamy Stock Photo:** John Gooday. **70-71 Alamy Stock Photo:** National Geographic Creative. **70 Alamy Stock Photo:** National Geographic Creative (l). **71 Alamy Stock Photo:** National Geographic Creative (tr). **73 Getty Images:** John Conrad. **74-75 Getty Images:** Murray Hayward. **76-77 Alamy Stock Photo:** Dominique Braud / Dembinsky Photo Associates. **78-79 FLPA:** D. Parer & E. Parer-Cook / Minden Pictures. **80 Getty Images:** Suzi Eszterhas / Minden Pictures. **82-83 iStockphoto.com:** Alphotographic. **84 Dorling Kindersley:** Cotswold Wildlife Park (bl, bc, br). **85 Dorling Kindersley:** Cotswold Wildlife Park (bl, br). **86-87 Alamy Stock Photo:** Nobuo Matsumura. **88-89 Alamy Stock Photo:** Life on white. **90-91 Getty Images:** Jeff Foott / Minden Pictures. **92-93 Alamy Stock Photo:** imageBROKER. **94 Alamy Stock Photo:** Miroslav Valasek. **96 123RF.com:** Giedrius Stakauskas (br). **Getty Images:** KeithSzafranski (l). **96-97 Dreamstime.com:** Jan Martin Will / Freezingpictures (b). **97 Dorling Kindersley:** Whipsnade Zoo (bc). **Dreamstime.com:** Inaras (br); Poeticpenguin (bc/Northern Rockhopper Penguin). **98-99 Dorling Kindersley:** Cotswold Wildlife Park. **102-103 naturepl.com:** Jen Guyton. **104-105 Alamy Stock Photo:** Eric Gevaert. **109 Getty Images:** Life On White. **112 Getty Images:** Digital Zoo. **114 Getty Images:** Roland Hemmi (cl). **114-115 Alamy Stock Photo:** Design Pics Inc (t). **117 Alamy Stock Photo:** Westend61 GmbH. **119 Getty Images:** Kevin Schafer. **120-121 123RF.com:** mirco1. **123 Alamy Stock Photo:** Picture Partners. **124 Getty Images:** Dave Fleetham. **127 iStockphoto.com:** Estivillml. **128 Dreamstime.com:** Isselee. **130-131 SuperStock:** Minden Pictures. **132 123RF.com:** Pumidol Leelerdsakulvong. **134 FLPA:** Matthias Breiter / Minden Pictures. **137 123RF.com:** Eric Isselee. **138-139 Getty Images:** Joel Sartore, National Geographic Photo Ark. **142-143 Alamy Stock Photo:** Matthijs Kuijpers. **148-149 Alamy Stock Photo:** All Canada Photos. **150-151 Getty Images:** www.tommaddick.co.uk. **152-153 FLPA:** Michael &, Patricia Fogden / Minden Pictures. **154-155 Alamy Stock Photo:** Robert Wyatt. **156 Eric Isselee (cla). Alamy Stock Photo:** Image Quest Marine (tc). **156-157 Dorling Kindersley:** Jerry Young (c). **158 naturepl.com:** Alex Mustard. **160 Andy Morffew. 162-163 Alamy Stock Photo:** Solvin Zankl. **165 Alamy Stock Photo:** Andia. **166 Alamy Stock Photo:** WaterFrame (clb). **166-167 Alamy Stock Photo:** cbimages (c). **167 Alamy Stock Photo:** Reinhard Dirscherl (clb). **Dorling Kindersley:** Linda Pitkin (tr). **iStockphoto.com:** Searsie (tl). **168-169 Alamy Stock Photo:** Life on White. **170 Getty Images:** ""Joel Sartore, National Geographic Photo Ark"""". **174-175 Alamy Stock Photo:** RGB Ventures. **176-177 Getty Images:** Visuals Unlimited, Inc. / Ken Catania. **178-179 Andy Morffew. 180-181 Dorling Kindersley:** Jerry Young. **182 naturepl.com:** Georgette Douwma. **184 123RF.com:** Dmytro Gilitukha (clb); Petr Kratochvil (ca). **Alamy Stock Photo:** Papilio (cla). **Dorling Kindersley:** Jerry Young (cb/Close-up, ca). **Getty Images:** Helen E. Grose (ca/Wings open). **iStockphoto.com:** Proxyminder (cl, fclb). **naturepl.com:** Stephen Dalton (fcla, cb, crb, fcrb, cr). **185 123RF.com:** Dmytro Gilitukha (tr); Aleksandrs Jemeljanovs (cla); Vaclav Krizek (cl); Petr Kratochvil (tc). **Dorling Kindersley:** Natural History Museum (ca); Jerry Young (c). **iStockphoto. com:** Proxyminder (cr). **naturepl.com:** Stephen Dalton (cra). **187 Dreamstime.com:** Petergyure. **189 Getty Images:** Alex Mustard / Nature Picture Library. **191 Alamy Stock Photo:** Zoonar GmbH. **192-193 Getty Images:** Jelger Herder / Buiten-beeld / Minden Pictures. **194-195 Dorling Kindersley:** Cotswold Wildlife Park. **198-199 Getty Images:** Barcroft Media. **200-201 Getty Images:** Joel Sartore. **202-203 FLPA:** Piotr Naskrecki / Minden Pictures. **204 Getty Images:** Tim Flach (tl, tc, ca, cra). **205 Getty Images:** Tim Flach (cl, b). **206-207 Alamy Stock Photo:** Blickwinkel. **208-209 Alamy Stock Photo:** Tomas Rak. **210-211 Alamy Stock Photo:** Photononstop. **212 Alamy Stock Photo:** Reinhard Dirscherl (bc/Starfish); Martin Strmiska (bl); Wildscotphotos (ca). **Dreamstime.com:** Musat Christian (ca/Beaver); Mikhail Blajenov / Starper (crl); Petergyure (crl/Kingfisher); Eric Isselee (cr); Yiu Tung Lee (br). **Fotolia:** uwimages (crb). **Getty Images:** www.tommaddick.co.uk (c). **naturepl.com:** Jen Guyton (cra). **213 Alamy Stock Photo:** Arco Images GmbH (bl); Life on White (cra, c); Nobuo Matsumura (cb/Octopus). **Dorling Kindersley:** Cotswold Wildlife Park (cb/Frog); Twan Leenders (cb); Jerry Young (crb, clb, cb/Scorpion). **Dreamstime. com:** Isselee (cr); Iakov Filimonov / Jackf (tl); Javarman (tc). **Getty Images:** Joel Sartore, National Geographic Photo Ark (cl); Joel Sartore (bc).

All other images © Dorling Kindersley
For further information see: www.dkimages.com